Forum Retreat
Planning Guide

◆ **Third Edition** ◆

forumsherpa

Forward

The Forum Retreat Planning Guide is a tool designed to assist anyone given the responsibility of planning their annual Forum retreat. The guide contains information about planning a retreat, what you can expect to accomplish during a retreat and an extensive collection of retreat exercises and activities to help keep your retreat fun, fresh and rewarding. While it is not necessary for everyone in your Forum to read the Forum Retreat Planning Guide, you may want to refer to specific sections and share them with your Forum members as they help with planning and logistics.

The guide is comprised of two parts. Part 1 explains the mechanics of a retreat – how to plan it, how to create an agenda, how to choose exercises and how to facilitate exercises. Part 2 provides a compilation of exercises, organized by category to use throughout your Forum retreat.

This book is typically used as a reference guide, so each section is designed to stand on its own. Readers are not expected to read the entire book cover to cover, but rather to access information if and when it's needed. A detailed Table of Contents is provided in the Preface and an Index is offered at the back of the book to assist you 11with locating vital information. If you are new to retreat planning, start by reading Part 1, especially sections 1 through 4.

Snapshot – Content Overview

Part 1: Retreat Planning Guide	Part 2: Forum Retreat Exercises
Chapters	**Categories**
1: Forum Retreat Basics	1: Retreat Openers
2: Retreat Planning: Objectives	2: Ice Breakers
3: Retreat Planning: Logistics	3: Forum Assessments
4: Retreat Planning: Agenda	4: Team Building
5: Running the Retreat	5: Building Team Spirit
6: Professional Facilitators	6: Business Exercises
7: Common Retreat Challenges	7: Personal Exercises
8: Wrapping Up the Retreat	8: Building Depth
	9: Retreat Closers

Copyrighted Materials

Forum Retreat Planning Guide, 3RD Edition

Permission is granted free of charge to photocopy the "worksheet" pages of this guide which are required for your Forum to complete the exercises herein. Only the original book purchaser may make such photocopies. Under no circumstances is it permitted to sell or distribute on a commercial basis material reproduced from this publication. Except as expressly provided herein, no part of this book may be reproduced or distributed in any form or by any means, or stored in a database retrieval system, without the prior written permission of the copyright owner. Permission may be obtained by contacting:

Publisher:

ForumSherpa, Inc.
Attn: Ellie Byrd
1087 Lewis River Rd., #227
Woodland, WA 98674

www.forumsherpa.com
info@forumsherpa.com

Printed in the United States of America   10 9 8 7 6 5 4 3 2 1

Forum Retreat Planning Guide – 3rd Edition

ISBN 13: 978-1930521209
ISBN 10: 1-9305-2120-0

Acknowledgments

People who write books of exercises must acknowledge the people they have never met. Facilitators, trainers, moderators and a host of creative people participate in a great oral tradition – someone makes up an exercise, they show it to someone else, other people adapt it, more people try it and over time it becomes an entity of its own, perhaps in many different forms. Sometimes, an exercise remains pure, as the creator intended it, and other times, it evolves into something different.

It is impossible to know or recognize all the people who may have been involved in the creation of a single exercise. Whenever someone has directly given us an exercise or idea for this book, we have made sure to give proper credit. When we were unsure or unable to verify the source of an exercise, the notation "Unknown" is used. We have not intentionally omitted recognition or altered the intent of any exercises. We welcome updates or corrections to our source information so that we may include proper recognition in future publications.

Special thanks to the people who contributed exercises directly to this book – Jorge Cherbosque, Bill Evans, Mo Fathelbab, Brigid Goldberg, Nancy Leach, Joan Mara, Francisco Puente, Terry Plochman, David Ryan and David Steel.

Recognition

Many others deserve thanks in many other ways. My heartfelt gratitude to the following people…

- To the team of dedicated facilitators who have used and/or tested many of these exercises – Maureen Schantz, Shelby Hacala, Mark Sanna, Jesus De La Garza, Dr. Mary Pike, John Cornelsen and Bob LaBonne.

- To Kate Millholland and Wayne Whitaker, for their tireless dedication to editing, layout and design. (Your patience with my endless changes knows no bounds!)

- To Jeb Stewart and Jill Archer, for providing me with the most beautiful place on the planet to do my most creative, focused and productive writing …

- To Nancy Cheek and Sheila Withrow, for your enduring friendship and unconditional love…

- To my dad, who is with me in spirit every day…

Table of Contents

Part 1 – Forum Retreat Planning Guide

Section 1 – Forum Retreat Basics

Section 2 – Retreat Planning: Objectives

Section 3 – Retreat Planning: Logistics

Section 4 – Retreat Planning: Agenda

Table of Contents

Table of Contents

Part 2 – Forum Retreat Exercises

Table of Contents

Table of Contents

Dedication

To my Forum…

For our 17-year journey together,

For the laughter and the tears,

For your unconditional love and support.

Thank you for being willing, curious and sometimes
painfully honest guinea pigs when I needed to try something out –

This book wouldn't exist without you!

Preface

Chapter 1
Forum Retreat Basics

Your annual Forum retreat is an important event in the continuous development of your Forum. The retreat is an opportunity to strengthen your bond as a Forum, to learn more about each other and to have fun!

This section contains basic information about holding your retreat. We'll look at a number of factors to consider when planning your retreat. 😳

What is a Forum Retreat?

The Forum Retreat is an annual event for everyone in your Forum. It provides a unique opportunity to learn, share, grow and accomplish specific objectives. Unlike Forum meetings, which typically focus on current issues and concerns, retreats have a longer-term view and delve into deeper issues. Therefore, the Forum retreat becomes an important element toward building depth and strengthening the overall Forum experience for members of the group.

Forum retreats include several key elements:

Elements of a Retreat

Work and Play

Two Overnight Stays

Mandatory Attendance

Work and Play Retreats should include a combination of work time and relaxation time. The balance depends on your Forum and the agreed-upon objectives for the Retreat. See Chapter 4 for more information on planning your agenda and how to determine the best balance of work time and play time.

Two Overnight Stays In order to be truly defined as a retreat, the Forum must include at least two overnight stays. Some retreats are three nights, four nights or as long as a week. In general, the longer the retreat, the more depth and bonding you can expect to accomplish with your Forum.

Mandatory Attendance Most Forums consider attendance at the annual retreat to be mandatory. Many Forums include a statement in their Forum norms/constitution that the retreat is required. If you miss it, you forfeit your membership in the Forum.

Note that planning is an essential element in a successful Forum retreat and, therefore, considerable information is included in Part 1 of this book on how to plan your retreat. Use this retreat guide as your roadmap in the planning process. Time permitting, you will gain the best benefit by reading all of Part 1, Sections 1 through 8. However, the sections are organized topically to help you find pertinent information as quickly as possible. 😳

What Are the Benefits of a Forum Retreat?

There are numerous benefits of holding a Forum retreat, which is why retreats are considered an annual staple for healthy Forums. First, retreats provide a fresh, new environment – a place away from the hectic pace that most business owners experience every day. By "getting away from it all", Forum members often find that they can shift to a new frame of mind.

Retreats are often a catalyst for change, inspiring big picture thinking and out-of-the-box ideas for people who may have limited time to focus on strategic issues. From a Forum perspective, the retreat is an opportunity to get to know each other better, increase depth in the Forum, and strengthen the bond between Forum members.

Many Forums use their annual retreat as an opportunity to assess their Forum health, update their Forum norms/constitution and set annual goals.

Here is a high-level list of the types of benefits your Forum can receive on a retreat:

- Build depth and intimacy in the Forum by getting to know each other better and sharing in a unique experience.

- Identify new ways to increase the value provided by the Forum to its members.

- Address and resolve Forum challenges and concerns.

- Learn about new topics that are of mutual interest to all Forum members.

- Provide a safe environment for people to take risks and share openly.

- Help a stale Forum revitalize itself, or help a strong Forum maintain its performance. ☺

Are There Any Risks In Having a Retreat?

Yes, there are potential downsides to a retreat, and it's wise to be aware of them and talk about them in advance.

First, when a Forum is struggling through a difficult time or difficult issues, the retreat can serve to bring the problems into the spotlight. In some cases, this can be uncomfortable and the situation may intensify. But in many cases, the results can be positive. By focusing on the challenges, the Forum has an opportunity to make changes and improve the situation. In the case of extreme challenges, your Forum may want to hire an outside facilitator to help your Forum navigate through the issue.

Note that retreats can make some people feel vulnerable. Emotions can be exposed and this can be somewhat uncomfortable, particularly for newer members. It's important that the Forum members have complete trust in confidentiality. When trust is not present, it may be difficult for the Forum to achieve its goals – both at the retreat and as a group.

Some people have difficulty being away from home, particularly when family or personal issues are a concern. A newborn baby or a sick child can cause stress. The retreat itself may be expensive, putting additional strain on a member with financial problems.

Retreats also take a toll on one of our most valuable assets – our time. Regardless of when the retreat is scheduled, or how far in advance it has been planned, there is never a perfect time for everyone. Some members may prefer that the retreat is scheduled during the week so it doesn't interfere with family time, while others may prefer

that it is held on the weekend so that it doesn't detract from work. A combination of the two may be a good compromise, and everyone in the Forum should be involved in scheduling the retreat. ☺

Who Should Attend?

Everyone in the Forum should attend the retreat. For many Forums, the retreat is mandatory with no exceptions. The reason for this is that retreats often result in an intense Forum growth experience that the absent member misses. The learning and growth cannot be recreated so there is no way to "catch up" after the event. If the absent member stays in the Forum, much of the progress that was made on the retreat may be lost, which is unfair to the rest of the group.

Only Forum members should attend the retreat—no spouses

> *... retreats often result in an intense bonding experience that the absent member misses. The event cannot be recreated so there is no way to catch up after the event.*

or significant others. Note that it is not acceptable for a spouse to stay in the hotel room while the member attends the retreat. The simple knowledge that a spouse is waiting in the room can put undue pressure on the member to hurry through exercises and/or want to end earlier in the evening. It also makes confidentiality seem less certain. For example, if something highly emotional or intense happens during the day, other members may feel less comfortable that confidentiality will be maintained with the spouse,

and, therefore, they may be less likely to open up. These concerns are the opposite of what we are trying to accomplish on the retreat.

A good alternative to having family members on the retreat is to invite them to arrive after the retreat is over, and stay on for an extra day or two. For those who can participate, it's a nice way to spend time with each other's families without causing distractions from the retreat itself.

What Makes a Great Retreat?

More than 100 Forums were surveyed in 2013 and asked about their retreat experience. The answers are a window into what makes a great retreat and what causes a bad experience. The top five answers are provided below for each question. Think about your retreat and consider how you can plan it to be in the BEST category.

Think of the BEST retreat your Forum has had. What made it so great?

- 43% - bonding with Forum members
- 39% - Forum activities – exercises and social
- 32% - specific location
- 26% - having an external facilitator
- 18% - being "unplugged"

Think of the WOSRT retreat your Forum has had. What made it so bad?

- 36% - agenda not well planned (lack of structure, goals)
- 23% - poor location
- 20% - poor member commitment (late, or no show)
- 19% - social activities pre-empted work
- 12% - too short

Cultural Sensitivity

If your Forum members come from multiple cultures, or if you are hiring a facilitator from another culture, be aware that perspectives, values and other differences may be inherently present. At the point where these differences collide, it's important to be understanding and receptive to differing viewpoints. Here is a short list of how some cultures vary.

- Some cultures value punctuality, adherence to schedules and accomplishing goals of the utmost importance while others value personal relationships and feelings.

- Some cultures value outward emotional expression while others value keeping emotions private.

- Some cultures are comfortable talking about intimate, personal details while others view this as inappropriate.

- Some cultures are comfortable with physical contact such as touching, hugs and pats on the back, while other cultures view physical contact as a violation of personal space.

- Some words have different meanings in different cultures, creating confusion for everyone when people interpret the same words differently.

- Body language varies between cultures. Hand gestures that are polite in one culture may be offensive in another culture. For example, nodding the heading can mean "Yes" in one culture and "No" in another.

One of the first aspects of cultural sensitivity is awareness. We must all recognize that cultural differences exist and that they are neither right or wrong, good or bad, they simply "are". When questions or concerns arise, it's best to talk about them openly and in a non-judgmental manner. The retreat ground rules will provide guidelines on how to do this effectively.

Resist the temptation to stereotype a person based on their cultural background. No behavior is common to all members of a culture and pre-determined biases are unfair and often inaccurate. ☺

Retreat Timeline

It's important to plan ahead if you want your retreat to be the best possible experience it can be. Ideally, start six months in advance and refer to the timeline below to be sure you're on track. Retreats that are put together at the last minute—one or two weeks before the retreat—are often unproductive and unfulfilling to the Forum.

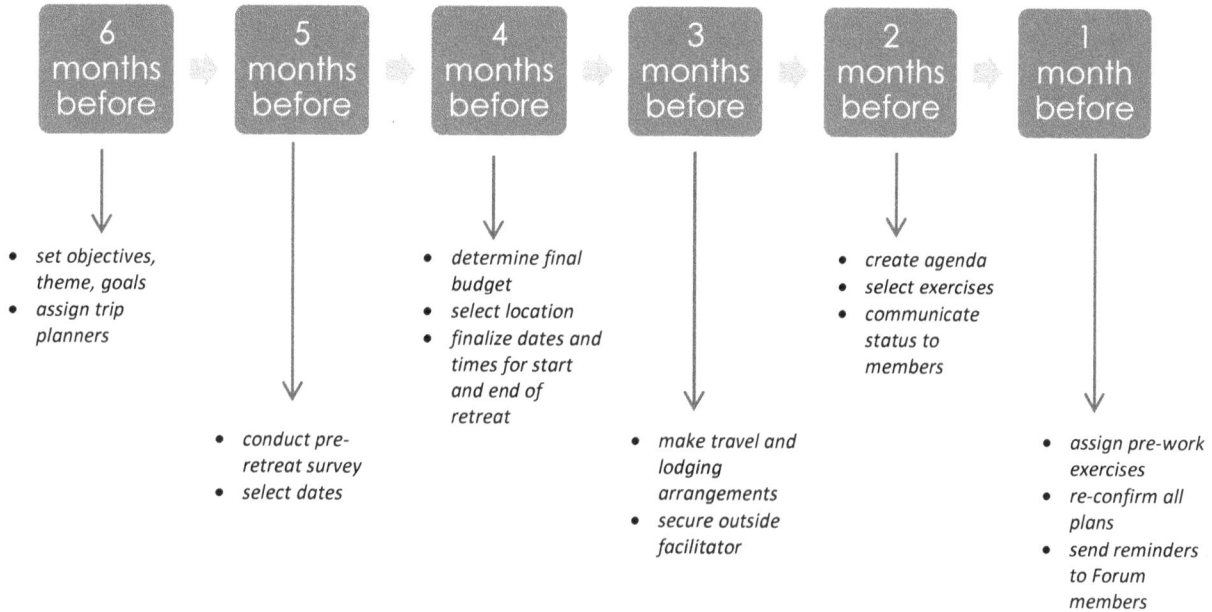

6 months before	5 months before	4 months before	3 months before	2 months before	1 month before

- set objectives, theme, goals
- assign trip planners

  - determine final budget
  - select location
  - finalize dates and times for start and end of retreat

    - create agenda
    - select exercises
    - communicate status to members

- conduct pre-retreat survey
- select dates

  - make travel and lodging arrangements
  - secure outside facilitator

    - assign pre-work exercises
    - re-confirm all plans
    - send reminders to Forum members

Retreat Planning Checklist

Logistics ☑

- ❏ Conduct pre-retreat survey
- ❏ Select retreat planners
- ❏ Select retreat dates
- ❏ Determine length of the retreat
- ❏ Determine budget
- ❏ Select a location
- ❏ Make lodging reservations
- ❏ Make meeting room reservations
- ❏ Make travel arrangements
- ❏ Determine sleeping arrangements
- ❏ Determine meal plans
- ❏ Assign financial responsibility

Activities ☑

- ❏ Identify primary goal(s) for the retreat
- ❏ Decide if you will hire a professional facilitator
- ❏ Make arrangements with the facilitator
- ❏ Prepare the retreat agenda
- ❏ Select exercises to support the primary goal
- ❏ Distribute pre-work (for exercises that require preparation)
- ❏ Select physical / fun activities
- ❏ Provide a list of what the members need to bring with them
- ❏ Arrange extra supplies (paper, flip charts, A/V, etc.)
- ❏ Determine roles and responsibilities for the retreat
- ❏ Create post-retreat evaluation
- ❏ Establish retreat ground rules

Chapter 2
Retreat Planning: Objectives

Deciding on the Outcome

As Stephen Covey says, "Begin with the end in mind". All Forum members should be involved in setting the objectives for the retreat. By making a collective decision, everyone can feel more comfortable that the retreat will be a worthwhile experience for them individually. Everyone understands that the objectives drive the activities and exercises, and they'll all be more inclined to fully participate during the retreat. This level of involvement also helps to build enthusiasm as the retreat approaches.

Finally, involve the participants in setting criteria for measuring the retreat's success. 😃

Setting Retreat Goals

Some of the most successful retreats focus on just one goal, and all activities during the retreat are singularly focused on achieving that goal. Multiple goals are fine, but be careful not to dilute what you are trying to accomplish. The retreat is limited in time so it must be limited in scope.

If you have conducted a Forum Health Survey (see Part 2, Retreat Exercises, Category 3, Forum Assessments), you may want to review the results and look for areas of interest or concern. This input can help guide your selection of a retreat goal.

Here are some ideas of goals you may want to consider for your retreat:

- integrate new members
- establish the Forum vision, mission and values
- improve Forum processes
- learn more about each other's businesses
- learn more about each other's personal lives
- stretch beyond our comfort zone
- improve life balance
- focus on a key topic (see Topical Retreats on the next page)

Organizational Health

If your Forum decides the primary purpose of the retreat is to work on the Forum itself, consider these seven areas of organizational health. Where might your Forum want to focus its efforts?

- Communication – internal communications, external communications, confidentiality, Gestalt Language Protocol

- Warmth and Support – openness, trust, depth of relationships

- Decisions – defined processes for achieving consensus, group norms/constitution

- Assets and Challenges – strengths, weaknesses, opportunities and threats as a group

- Benefits and Rewards – increasing the value of the Forum experience

- Organizational Clarity – roles and responsibilities, processes, agenda

- Team Spirit – commitment to the Forum, understanding diversity, sharing goals, integrating new members

Note that a major discrepancy over the retreat goals can be an important reflection of deeper problems within the Forum. In one Forum, several members wanted to go on a beach vacation where casinos and alcohol were readily available. They wanted a stress-free, fun vacation with their Forum buddies. Other members were more interested in building Forum depth and expanding their business knowledge. Ultimately, this Forum decided to split. Each group then expanded to bring in new members who shared their own objectives for the Forum experience. 🌐

Topical Retreats

Your Forum may have a topic of mutual interest to all Forum members. Experts and curriculum abound in all of these areas. Exploring the topic can become the central theme of your retreat. Exercises and activities can focus on the topic, bringing strength and continuity to the retreat agenda. Here are some ideas to get you started:

- leadership development
- business exit strategies
- strategic planning
- personnel issues
- marriage
- spirituality
- health
- relationship with parents
- relationship with children
- financial planning
- life balance

🌐

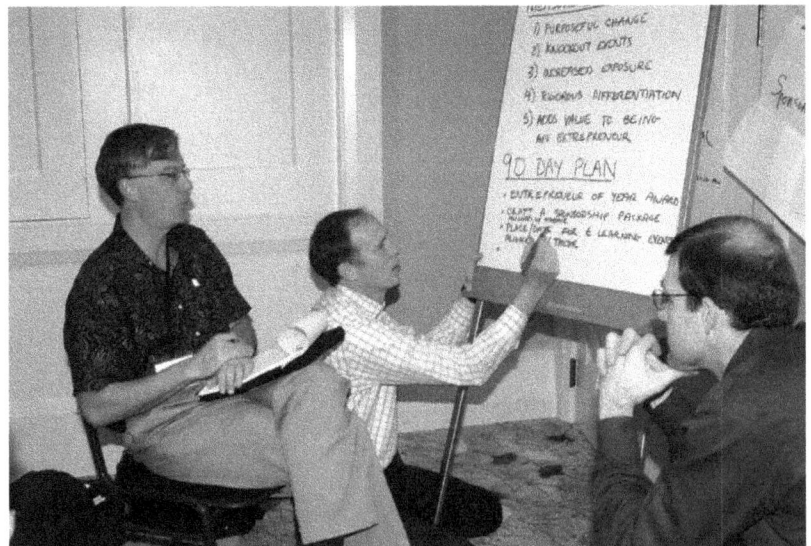

Behavioral Assessments

Behavioral assessments are a tool to help us learn more about ourselves and about each other. They can spark discussions about individual styles and personality traits. They can identify group dynamics that may be affecting how your Forum functions as a cohesive team. Some Forums include a behavioral assessment in their retreat once every few years as a means of self-analysis and group development.

Most professional assessments have certification programs for trainers and facilitators. Ideally, bring in a facilitator who is an expert on the assessment you are using to guide you through the interpretation process. A trained facilitator can also provide credibility and guidance without personal bias.

There are a variety of group dynamics assessments and 360° assessments also available. For best results, discuss what you are trying to accomplish with your Forum, then decide which assessment is the best fit for your objectives. 😊

Personality Assessments

- DISC Personality Profile
- Myers-Briggs Type Indicator® (MBTI®)
- Kolbe Index
- Hartmann Value Profile
- Birkman Method® Assessment
- Lominger Leadership Assessment
- Dave Kurlan Sales Assessment
- Type A Personality Test

Assigning Retreat Planners

Planning the retreat is a big job, and different parts of the planning process require different skills. Getting two or more Forum members involved in planning has several benefits.

- Two brains are better than one – having multiple people involved brings more ideas and creativity to the planning process.
- The workload for each person is lighter when shared.
- Concerns are alleviated that one individual is operating in a silo.
- Members have more buy-in on the retreat plans.

A common scenario for sharing the workload is to have a team of retreat planners, preferably made up of three people. The work can be divided as follows:

Role	Responsibility
Logistics	Responsible for arranging all transportation, lodging, meeting room, sleeping arrangements, meals, snacks, drinks, reservations, communications.
Work Time	Responsible for selecting all content for the retreat, including pre-work exercises, onsite exercises, printed materials and facilitator selection.
Play Time	Responsible for arranging all fun activities, including games, physical activities and relaxation time.

Assigning Retreat Planners, continued

Ideally, the retreat planners will begin the planning process six months before the retreat. Together, they will construct the agenda and handle a wide variety of aspects regarding the retreat. They can bounce ideas off of each other and coordinate their efforts to create the most powerful retreat experience for the Forum. At each Forum meeting, the retreat planners can report on their progress and get input on various issues as needed. This type of regular communication helps build momentum and enthusiasm among the Forum members.

Note that the retreat planners are not responsible for running the retreat, although they are welcome to do so. In some cases, the moderator or the moderator-elect will run the retreat, with assistance from the retreat planners and the other members. In other cases, a professional facilitator may be hired to run the retreat. These decisions should be made in advance of the retreat so that people can adequately prepare for their role. 🌐

Keeping Members Updated

Throughout the planning process, the Retreat Planners should provide an update to the rest of the Forum on their progress. This can be handled in the Housekeeping section of the Forum meeting, or it may be a separate agenda item in the meeting. In addition to keeping everyone informed, the updates serve to build consensus and enthusiasm about the retreat.

Take advantage of this great way to keep everyone involved and excited about the retreat! 🌐

Chapter 3
Retreat Planning: Logistics

Pre-Retreat Survey

A pre-retreat survey is a valuable tool to gather information from your Forum members on their preferences for the retreat. You can discuss the survey openly, or you can ask people to complete the survey and then compile the results offline. A written survey can be open or anonymous. The advantage to an open survey is that you can engage in an open discussion about individual responses. The advantage to an anonymous survey is that people are more apt to answer questions candidly. For example, someone who is having financial problems may be hesitant to argue for a low retreat budget in an open survey. But in an anonymous survey, they can state their preference boldly.

A sample survey of ten basic questions is provided below. Feel free to adjust the questions to fit your Forum and your needs. 😊

Sample Pre-Retreat Survey

1) Rate each of the following goals on a scale of 1 (low) to 10 (high) as to whether you would like them to be a focal point for the retreat. Feel free to add your own goals suggestions at the end.

   a. Get to know Forum members better.
   b. Integrate new members into the Forum.
   c. Improve members' listening and communication skills.
   d. Spend introspective time on self-development.
   e. Improve our Presentation process.
   f. Overhaul our Forum norms/constitution.
   g. Become a better business leader.
   h. <add your own goal ideas>

2) Select the budget range that is most comfortable for you.

   a. under $1000
   b. $1000 to $2500
   c. $2500 to $5000
   d. $5000 to $10,000
   e. don't care

3) What climate is preferable to you?

   a. warm
   b. cool
   c. don't care

Sample Pre-Retreat Survey, continued

4) What is the maximum travel time acceptable to you?

   a. driving distance
   b. less than 1 hour flight time
   c. less than 2 hours flight time
   d. less than 3 hours flight time
   e. doesn't matter

5) How many nights are you willing/able to be away for the retreat?

   a. 1 night only
   b. 2 nights
   c. 3 nights
   d. doesn't matter

6) What types of extra-curricular activities interest you? (check all that apply)

   a. golfing
   b. hiking
   c. white water rafting
   d. boating / sailing
   e. skiing
   f. sleeping
   g. horseback riding
   h. skin diving
   i. ropes course
   j. rock climbing
   k. sight-seeing tour
   l. museum tour

7) How would you like our exercises to be facilitated?

   a. facilitation handled by moderator
   b. facilitation shared by all members
   c. facilitation handled by a paid professional facilitator

8) Do you have any dietary restriction, allergies, or special physical needs that we should be aware of? If yes, please describe.

   a. yes _____
   b. no

Sample Pre-Retreat Survey, continued

9) What concerns, if any, do you have about the retreat? What should we avoid on this retreat?

_____

_____

10) What could we do to make this retreat the most valuable possible experience for you? What would make this retreat a WOW experience?

_____

_____

This type of survey is specifically about the retreat and it should be distinguished from a Forum Health survey. Many Forums also conduct an annual Forum Health survey, and just before the retreat can be a good time to do this. The Forum can use the retreat to review the results of the Forum Health survey and discuss issues of concern. There are several sample Forum Health surveys provided in Part 2 of this book.

Setting the Retreat Dates and Retreat Length

Forum retreats can be held at any time of year. Most Forums try to steer away from holidays when family events are prominent, and summertime when family vacations are often planned. Many Forums choose a particular time of year, such as the Spring season, and consistently schedule their retreats at that time of year. This becomes an expectation of the Forum members and it's less likely that the retreat will be missed.

The length of the retreat is another decision point. You will need to factor in the objectives of the retreat, the complexity of the issues to be addressed, the availability of your Forum members and the financial cost. In order for the event to be defined as a retreat, a minimum

of two overnight stays must be included. A retreat that is three nights long is generally a better length to consider. Be sure you allot enough time to accomplish the retreat goals, otherwise, people may leave feeling frustrated that the retreat was a poor use of their time and ultimately, unsuccessful.

> *Holding retreats regularly, once per year, is a best practice for Forums to follow.*

Generally, the longer the retreat, the more you can expect to accomplish. Retreats that span two or more full days allow participants ample time to shift their mental focus off of daily details and explore deeper,

more strategic issues more thoroughly. However, a retreat that is too long could be detrimental. Retreats require that members are fully present – mentally, emotionally and physically – and the intense focus can become draining at some point. Don't overdo it.

One cautionary point for some Forums is a situation where the retreat is repeatedly delayed or rescheduled. Attendance at the retreat is a reflection of the members' commitment to the Forum, and the retreat itself is a powerful component of a healthy Forum. Holding retreats regularly, once per year, is a best practice for Forums to follow. If this is not happening, it could be a sign of deeper problems within the Forum. One idea to get back on track if your

Setting the Retreat Dates and Retreat Length, continued

Forum has missed one or more retreats is to schedule a one-day mini-retreat as soon as possible and bring in a professional Forum facilitator to run the program. With the help of a facilitator, focus on

Forum health as the main topic. Afterwards, the Forum may find renewed commitment to schedule a full retreat. ☻

Setting the Budget

Everyone's budgetary constraints must be considered when planning the retreat. There is a common phrase – "The Forum is only as rich as its poorest member." This means we can't force a Forum member to pay more for the retreat than they can reasonably afford.

Creative financing can be done, where a member who is financially able and willing could cover the cost of a specific part of the retreat. For example, one member might provide their summer villa for accommodations, or provide a charter jet for transportation, or pay for a group excursion on a sailboat. Another idea is to allow financially able members to contribute to a pool that helps those who are financially strapped. However, this practice can have risky side effects because the relationships change as a result.

For example...

Consider the case of Joe, a Forum member who was struggling with his business and felt he couldn't afford the retreat unless they stayed at a member's lake house within driving distance. Several other members offered to cover the cost of Joe's expenses so that the group could travel to another country for a more elaborate retreat. Everyone seemed fine with the arrangement until a few months after the retreat when Joe bought himself a new sports car. Suddenly, the people who helped subsidize Joe's retreat cost felt used and angry.

Some Forums use money from fines to help subsidize the retreat. Fines are typically assessed to members throughout the year for various infractions of the Forum norms/constitution, such as being late for a meeting, forgetting to turn off their cell phone, etc.

Gathering people's budgetary preferences can be done through a survey, in an open discussion, or in private discussions with the moderator. Be considerate of people who may be embarrassed of their current financial situation, particularly new members who may not yet be comfortable discussing finances. Bottom line, be sure everyone has the opportunity to express their financial preferences and arrive at a group consensus on what the final budget will be. ☻

Paying for the Retreat

The Forum should clearly discuss how finances will be handled on the retreat in advance.

In some Forums, one person will pay for everything, then divvy up the charges for everyone afterwards. In other Forums, everyone pays individually as the expenses are incurred. Still other Forums will use a hybrid combination where different people pay for different things. After the retreat, expenses are submitted to the Treasurer who calculates who owes what to whom.

Before embarking on your retreat, decide on the following:

- How will costs be split among Forum members?
- Who will pay for activities and meals during the retreat?
- Will receipts be required in order to get reimbursed from the Forum?
- Will the Forum kitty be used to pay for retreat expenses?
- Will anyone pay a different amount than the others? For example, someone might want to pay extra for a first class airline ticket. Someone else who doesn't drink alcohol might not want to contribute to the alcohol purchases.
- How soon after the retreat should receipts be turned in?
- How soon after the retreat will everyone pay up and be paid?

Deciding on these and any other financial issues are best handled in advance.

Choosing the Location

The location of the retreat is critical to its success. Getting away from your everyday, normal environment provides the opportunity for more relaxed, creative, analytical thinking. Familiar venues can be reminders of current, daily issues whereas retreats are intended to be a respite from daily drudgeries. Therefore, attempt to avoid local places that are too close to home.

Distractions should be minimized if not eliminated. Some Forums go to a location where cell phones don't work, or everyone agrees to turn their cell phones off throughout the retreat. Providing a central phone number (hotel main desk, cottage main line) can generally suffice for emergencies. Even more

extreme is to go to a place where television and radio are not available. This can provide a peaceful sanctuary where the Forum can achieve a high level of focus.

Consider the objective of the retreat when selecting your location. Do you need formal meeting room space? Audio/video capabilities? Internet access? Do you want a place that is serene or full of energy? Do you want access to a particular type of sport or activity?

The wrong location can set the wrong tone for the retreat. For example, if your retreat is intended to focus on business issues, then a camping trip where meeting rooms aren't available could be clumsy. If the

retreat is to study family relationships, then staying at a casino is probably not the best environment.

Retreats tend to work best in comfortable, flexible environments where the Forum can be relaxed and casual. The location doesn't have to be fancy or expensive. In fact, a posh resort may distract people from the work at hand.

Choosing the Location, continued

One of the most popular choices is to rent a large house or a villa where the Forum can stay under one roof. This option provides a shared living space, a built-in meeting location and the opportunity to experience everyday life together, such as casual conversation, impromptu discussions, cooking meals, etc. An added advantage is that home rentals are often more economical than hotel rooms. Some Forums hire a chef or a caterer to prepare meals thanks to the cost savings.

There are hotels and conference centers around the globe that are designed to handle small meeting groups. Also, consider resorts and lodges in their off-season, such as a ski resort in summer or a beach house in winter. They often have a beautiful setting, they're less crowded, and they're generally less expensive in the off-season.

Yet another option is to use a summer home of one of the Forum members. If you choose this option, be sure the member is adequately compensated for the use of staples, utilities, cleaning services, etc. ☺

Determining Travel Plans

Ideally, traveling should be part of the retreat. The retreat starts when you leave your home city. If you are flying somewhere, fly together on the same flight. If you are driving somewhere, rent a mini-van or an RV and drive together.

There are several reasons to travel together. One, you can engage in exercises--fun or serious exercises--during the travel time. Also, by traveling together, we avoid potential problems with someone arriving late, getting lost or running into travel problems on their own. Finally, you learn about each other by travelling together! The retreat closes when you return to your home city.

If travelling together isn't possible, try to minimize travel time and combine your travel plans as much as possible. Most importantly, be sure that everyone arrives at the designated location in time for the start of the retreat.

If people are driving, be sure each driver has clear, accurate information on where they are going, especially if you are travelling to a remote location. One person arriving late can derail the agenda, give everyone a sour taste and start the retreat off on a bad note. ☺

Determining Sleeping Arrangements

Travel Together

Stay Together

Work Together

Play Together

The best possible locations are places where the entire Forum can stay under the same roof, have private sleeping rooms but shared meeting areas. This can be accomplished in several ways – at a villa, a cabin, a large house, on a large boat, a bed & breakfast, etc.

Another possible location is a hotel. Attempt to arrange for your rooms to be together--adjacent to each other or at least on the same floor. Be sure to make arrangements for meeting space. Perhaps you can rent suites for several people to share that will offer a shared living area that can double as a meeting room.

Sharing rooms is a common practice, and it saves money. The topic should be discussed with the entire Forum to be sure everyone is comfortable. Of course, male and female members stay in separate rooms. ☺

Meeting Room Details

Some of the most obvious details of a meeting room are sometimes overlooked. A little advance planning can ensure that creature comforts are met. If you are staying at a facility that offers meeting rooms, use this Meeting Room Checklist. If you are staying in a less formal environment, attempt to follow the same guidelines and adjust as necessary to suit the location.

Meeting Room Checklist

- Select a meeting room that ensures confidentiality can be maintained.

- Ask if the room has windows. A closed room with no windows can feel confining after a while.

- Find out what types of chairs are in the room. Rolling chairs with arms are far more comfortable than armless chairs that aren't on wheels.

- Be sure the room temperature can be controlled at a comfortable level. Wear layered clothing and bring a small fan if needed!

- Arrange the room so that everyone can see each other. A round table is ideal as it puts everyone on an even plane. A rectangular board table can also work. Avoid a U-shaped setup which separates people more. Note that some Forums prefer to have no table at all, but rather a circle of comfortable chairs. Removing the table completely removes a physical barrier and this, in turn, can encourage more openness and free-flowing communications.

- If possible, change the room setup or at least have people change seats between each block of exercises. (A block is a morning or an afternoon of exercises.) A fresh perspective means better attention.

- If you need audio-visual aids such as a projector, screen, flip charts, white board, CD player, etc., be sure to arrange these amenities in advance or bring them with you.

- Clarify whether the room will be yours for the entire retreat. Can you leave your materials in the room overnight? Can you leave flip chart paper on the walls and know that it will be there in the morning? Or will you need to vacate the room completely after each session?

Meeting Room Details, continued

If your retreat is at a hotel, consider a large hospitality suite rather than a traditional meeting room. Suites often provide more room, more comfortable seating, natural light from windows, and access to a kitchen where drinks and snacks can be available all day. Suites also tend to offer more privacy than a bank of meeting rooms that can be noisy and distracting. One or more Forum members may be able to stay in the suite for added cost savings. ☺

Dress Code

In most cases, the dress code for the retreat is casual, for example, blue jeans, shorts, t-shirts, etc. The casual dress and relaxed offsite environment can provide a comfortable setting to inspire openness and creativity. Of course, depending on the venue where you are holding your retreat, the dress code may be dictated for you. If you are on a tropical island, or skiing in the mountains, you will need to adjust your wardrobe accordingly. Some resorts require specific dress codes in certain places, for example, a sport jacket or a tie may be required for dining in a particular restaurant.

Always remember to check the weather forecast before packing to be sure you bring appropriate clothes for the climate. If you will be spending time in meeting rooms, remember that these rooms are often cool and a light sweater or jacket may be helpful. ☺

Food and Drink

For your main meals, you can dine out, order in, or make your own. If you are staying in a house or a lodge where a kitchen is available, you could consider cooking meals together as a fun, team exercise. Or you could assign one meal to each person, or hire a chef, or order out.

If you are going to eat out, make reservations in advance so that you won't waste time waiting for a large table at a busy restaurant. Consider the atmosphere, the noise level and the cost of your restaurant choices. Also, consider the serving speed. If you are pressed for time, a slow seven-course dinner may not be suitable.

For daytime food (during your meetings), consider the following suggestions:

- Have "brain food" available during "work" time, rather than heavy sweets or carbohydrate snacks. Here is a short list of foods that will help keep people thinking smart!

    - *fresh fruits*
    - *fresh vegetables*
    - *raw nuts*
    - *assorted proteins such as cheese, yogurt, shrimp or meat*

- Be sure plenty of water is available. Staying hydrated keeps the mind alert.

- Plan mid-morning and mid-afternoon snack breaks to refuel the mind and body.

Food and Drink, continued

- Keep breakfast and lunch fairly light to avoid sleepiness.

- If possible, try to schedule lunch in a separate room from the meeting space. This gives people both a physical and a mental break from the meeting room.

For alcohol, determine people's preferences and decide if you will bring alcohol to the retreat and/or buy alcohol on site. A candid discussion about alcohol consumption is wise. There should be set times on the retreat agenda where alcohol is allowed, generally in the evenings after all serious Forum exercises are done.

Also, discuss the volume of alcohol consumed. Drinking to excess can cause many problems – from illness to missed sessions the next morning. Raise awareness of this potential problem and attempt to diffuse it before it happens.

Finally, check with everyone in advance to see if there are any special dietary needs or preferences. Select foods and restaurants that can accommodate these needs so that everyone is comfortable. ☺

Cell Phones and Electronic Devices

In today's age of technology, instant connection and global access, policies for electronic devices abound. In the spirit of mutual respect, focus, and introspection that Forums typically seek on a retreat, the use of technology is discouraged. The opportunity to be completely unplugged can be refreshing, relaxing and inspirational.

Turning off technology may not work for all people or all Forums. Have a conversation about the use of electronics before the retreat, let all voices be heard and decide on an acceptable policy for the retreat. Consider taking an anonymous vote on the policy. Often, a combination of using technology and abstaining from technology during specific times may be a reasonable compromise.

Discuss the usage of cameras, photos, videos and social media postings. Are these things permissible? Be sure everyone is clear and comfortable with the policy in advance. Unexpected postings online have been the source of problems on some Forum retreats. The problem can be easily avoided with clear communications up front. ☺

Chapter 4
Retreat Planning: Agenda

Creating An Agenda

One of the most important aspects of a successful retreat is developing a clear and thoughtful agenda. The retreat's agenda should outline the objectives of the retreat and the sessions to be covered. Assigning times to agenda items helps keep exercises on schedule, but don't try to tackle too much in any given session. Setting priorities for your agenda and sticking to them will help you use your retreat time well, but be flexible enough to explore innovative ideas or unrecognized issues if they arise.

You may want to start with a blank sheet of paper and write down all the exercises and activities you want to accomplish during the retreat. Then, based on the length of your retreat, begin assigning various activities to specific time blocks. Try to have a healthy variety of activities each day and be sure you include enough time for breaks, changing clothes, driving to different locations, etc.

If you are hiring a professional facilitator to help you run the retreat, determine how involved they will be in creating the agenda. Some facilitators will create the entire agenda for you. Other facilitators will provide content during specific times that you have designated on the agenda. In either case, be sure the facilitator is familiar with the agenda. They need to know what is happening before and after their sessions, where the energy level will be during their sessions, and which times are fixed and which are more flexible. ☺

The Right Balance – Work and Play

Possible Balance of Work Time and Play Time

Work	Play
70%	30%
60%	40%
50%	50%
40%	60%
30%	70%

The balance between work and play will probably vary at each of your retreats. A significant factor is what you want to accomplish on the retreat. For example, if the retreat is all about business development, then you will probably spend more time at work than play. If the retreat is all about bonding and building interpersonal relationships, then you will probably spend more time on relaxing and non-structured activities rather than work. Discuss the balance with your Forum before you plan the agenda. Try to settle on a percentage of how the time should be split.

If you're not sure how to split your time, start at 50/50 and work out from there. Try not to go more than 70/30 in either direction. The Forum needs to get some business value on the retreat. The Forum also needs to spend time building interpersonal relationships. Both are important!

To maximize your time, you may want to consider assigning a discussion topic for one or two of your meals. Don't overdo this,

The Right Balance – Work and Play, continued

because down time is important and free-flowing conversations are healthy for the Forum. But this can be an effective, timely way to address lighter issues. After the meal, review the discussion and make note of any action items or decisions that were made.

On the flip side, be sure there is some "white space" included in the agenda. This is time when there is nothing scheduled—neither work nor play. It's free time with no imposed structure. Sometimes, meaningful conversations and important introspection take place during the white space, so it's wise to allow for this.

The examples provided below are intended to give you an idea of how your retreat could be organized. Feel free to adjust the times, exercises, activities and meals to suit your Forum. ☺

Sample Agenda, 1-Night Retreat (Mini-Retreat)

Retreats that include only one night are often called mini-retreats. They may be used mid-year (between annual retreats) to refresh, re-energize and refocus. Note that two nights is considered the minimum length of a standard annual Forum retreat.

Day 1	Day 2
11:00am Arrive, check-in, lunch	8:00am Breakfast
12:30pm Forum exercises	9:00am Forum exercises
5:00pm Free time	10:30am Fun, physical activity
6:30pm Dinner	1:00pm Lunch
8:30pm Introspective exercise	2:00pm Forum exercises
	6:00pm Retreat closing

Sample Agenda, 2-Night Retreat

Day 1	Day 2	Day 3
6:00pm Arrive, dinner 8:30pm Relaxation time	8:00am Breakfast 9:00am Forum exercises 1:00pm Lunch 2:00pm Fun, physical activity 6:00pm Dinner 8:30pm Introspective exercise	8:00am Breakfast 9:00am Forum exercises 12:00pm Fun activity 1:00pm Lunch 2:00pm Forum exercises 5:00pm Retreat closing

Sample Agenda, 3-Night Retreat

Day 1	Day 2	Day 3	Day 4
6:00pm Arrive, dinner 8:30pm Relaxation time	8:00am Breakfast 9:00am Forum exercises 1:00pm Lunch 2:00pm Forum exercises 6:00pm Dinner 8:30pm Introspective exercise	8:00am Breakfast 9:00am Fun day-long activity 6:00pm Dinner 8:30pm Relaxation	8:00am Breakfast 9:00am Forum exercises 1:00pm Retreat closing

Choosing Exercises

At the beginning of the retreat, people tend to be more distracted by thoughts from work, family, recent events, etc. They are also more guarded with their openness. Therefore, it is usually better to start the retreat with more cognitive types of exercises and move toward more introspective, depth exercises later in the retreat.

The key driving factor behind the exercises you choose is the retreat goal. Select exercises that support the goal and you will be more likely to achieve the goal.

There are many sources of exercises:

- Part 2 of this book offers a wide variety of retreat exercises, including instructions and time required.

- Talk to other Forums and ask them which exercises have been most useful to them.

- Ask your Forum members if they have used exercises at other retreats, perhaps with their own company.

- Purchase a book of retreat exercises.

- Hire a facilitator to bring in their own exercises.

- Purchase exercises from a facilitator.

Here is an example of exercises and activities for two different retreat goals. Underlined items are included in Part 2 of this book.

Goal: Build Forum depth & commitment		Goal: Focus on Sales & Marketing	
Exercise	That 's Incredible	Exercise	Topical Discussion on Marketing practices
Exercise	Build a new Parking Lot		
Learning	Review coaching and presentation process	Exercise	Sales Call – each member shares their sales & marketing plan, marketing materials
Exercise	Cross-coaching		
Exercise	30-minute presentations (all members present on an issue)	Activity	Golf competition
		Exercise	Brainstorming session – one member's Sales challenge
Activity	Ropes Course (builds trust)		
Exercise	Who Am I	Video	Killer Sales and Marketing
Exercise	High Hurdles	Demo	Member demo of www.salesforce.com
Activity	Reflection Walk		
Exercise	Topical Discussion on Life Balance	External Expert	Hired to present on Motivating Your Sales Force
		Activity	Sailboat dinner cruise
		Exercise	Embarrassing Moments

Choosing Exercises, continued

Also, note that it is acceptable for one or two members give a formal Presentation on the retreat. Be sure these people have met with a coach and/or have properly prepared for their Presentation, just as they would for a regular Forum meeting. 😃

Forum Retreat Exercises

Part 2 of this book consists of Forum Retreat Exercises. These exercises are specifically designed to be used by Forums. Exercises are divided into categories to simplify the process of selecting appropriate exercises for your retreat. Times are estimated based on a 8-person Forum, so you will need to adjust the times if your Forum has more or fewer members.

Category	Description of Exercises
1. Retreat Openers	Use these exercises at the beginning of the retreat to set expectations and ground rules.
2. Ice Breakers	Use these exercises early in the retreat (or each morning) to loosen up, lighten up and have fun.
3. Forum Assessments	Use an assessment to gauge the health of your Forum. Many Forums conduct an assessment each year to measure progress and identify opportunities for improvement.
4. Team Building	Use these exercises to work on the Forum itself. Team-building exercises can help integrate new members and re-invigorate existing members.
5. Building Team Spirit	Everyone has different skills and styles. Fun exercises can help us find ways to work together, reach consensus and build productive relationships.
6. Business Exercises	Use these exercises to explore business issues and strategies. Each member reflects on the specific topic first, then presents back to the Forum.
7. Personal Exercises	Use these exercises for introspective thinking. Each member analyzes themselves first, then shares their thoughts and self-discoveries with the Forum. Members learn about themselves, learn from each other and learn about each other.
8. Building Depth	These exercises are more intense. They generally require pre-work before the retreat and they involve deep, introspective thinking. These exercises require a high level of trust in confidentiality and a safe, non-judgmental environment to be effective.
9. Retreat Closers	Use these exercises at the end of the retreat to review the retreat and bring it to a comfortable close.

Choosing Fun Activities

There are a wide variety of activities that you can include on your retreat. First, talk with your Forum to decide on the level of physical activity and excitement they want. Do you want more sedentary activities like fishing and sight-seeing tours, or more strenuous activities like rock climbing and skydiving? Look at what's available in the location where your retreat will be held. In fact, the activities may drive the selection of your retreat location.

Next, decide if there are activities that support the overall goal of the retreat.

For example, if your retreat is focused on building trust in the Forum, then a high ropes course or white-water rafting excursion would be appropriate. If your retreat is focused on life balance and stress reduction, you may want to go on a nature hike in the mountains or take a hot yoga class.

Finally, be sure you select activities in which all members can participate. For example, if one of your members has back trouble and can't go horseback riding, then that's not an appropriate activity for the retreat. Everyone should be included in all activities. ☺

Ideas of Fun Activities

Fishing	Canoeing	Cooking school
Golfing	Kayaking	Spa
Sailing	Outward Bound program	Museum tour
Swimming	Zip-lining	Art class
Bowling	High ropes course	Boat tour
Low ropes course	Skiing	Walking tour
Hunting	Skydiving	Miniature golf
Horseback riding	White-water rafting	Habitat for Humanity project
Cycling	Rock climbing	Bungee jumping
Dude ranch	Paint-ball	Scavenger hunt

Assigning Pre-Work

Pre-work involves preparation time before the retreat that will enable the time spent together on the retreat to have the highest possible value. Pre-work can consist of preparatory exercises, reading assignments, surveys, assessments or diary logs.

The pre-work should be completed before the retreat. Based on the agenda you have created, determine which exercises require pre-work. Be sure to distribute the pre-work at least one month before the retreat to give everyone plenty of time to complete the work. Also, be sure to include specific instructions so that people understand what they're supposed to do.

How much pre-work is appropriate? Generally, somewhere between 1 hour and 4 hours of pre-work for a retreat can be expected. Depending on the objectives of the retreat, this number may be higher. Everyone should be aware of the amount of pre-work expected and everyone must be willing and able to commit the time.

Encourage people to complete their pre-work well before the retreat starts. Too often, people wait until the night before the retreat, then they either find themselves rushed or they don't have the information they need to complete the exercise. This is frustrating and unfair to other Forum members who have taken the time and effort to complete their work well in advance.

Worse yet, if people arrive at the retreat without their pre-work done, entire exercises can become obsolete and the ripple effect can derail the entire retreat agenda. Be sure everyone understands the importance of completing their pre-work in advance. 🌐

Agenda Adjustments On-Site

While the agenda is a critical component to a successful retreat, always keep the retreat objectives in mind. Achieving the objective is more important than following the agenda to the minute. At times, a diversion from the retreat may be necessary and healthy in order to accomplish the objective. A spontaneous discussion may address issues better than some of the planned exercises. The group should feel comfortable making an intentional adjustment to the agenda to accommodate this, under the leadership of their moderator or facilitator. 🌐

Mini-Retreats

Note that some Forums engage in a mini-retreat midyear between the regular annual retreats. This is typically a one day, 12-hour session, so plan on 8am to 8pm, or 9am to 9pm, etc. Have your meals together, work on exercises together, bring in a facilitator or an expert for part of the retreat, and schedule some fun time. This can be a good, mid-year boost for your Forum. The location is not as important because the bulk of the retreat will be spent on topical exercises rather than extra-curricular activities. Select a comfortable, local meeting room, but do not use a member's office meeting room. Everyone needs to get away from familiar surroundings for the optimum retreat experience, even on a mini-retreat. 🌐

Setting Retreat Ground Rules

Setting ground rules for your retreat in advance can help avert problems before they arise. Ground rules set expectations for acceptable behaviors and help to keep discussions focused. Here is a list of topics to consider and discuss as a group before the retreat begins.

External Communications	Cell phones, laptops and other electronic devices – How will they be handled throughout the retreat?
Communication Style	Consider a list of preferred communication techniques during work exercises: • Be fully present. • Let one person speak at a time. Don't interrupt. • Don't engage in side conversations or inside jokes. • Listen intently. • Treat each other with respect. • Listen to understand, not to judge. • Be willing to take a risk. Share openly.
Decisions	Discuss and determine how decisions will be made and how disagreements will be handled -- consensus, majority rule or "what the leader says goes."
Confidentiality	What aspects of the retreat are considered confidential? Is it okay to talk about fun aspects of the retreat?
Alcohol	How much alcohol is appropriate to consume? Are there any concerns about other substances that should be addressed?

Chapter 5
Running the Retreat

Who Should Run the Retreat?

Running the retreat is an important job. It involves managing the agenda, starting and ending activities, handling issues as they arise, and being the point person for whatever happens. The person in charge must be constantly aware of timing, empathetic to all the Forum members, and ready to make adjustments as needed.

You have several choices for who runs the retreat:

- The moderator can run the entire retreat.

- The moderator-elect can run the retreat.

- The trip planner(s) can run the entire retreat.

- Different segments of the retreat can be assigned to different members of the Forum so that everyone is involved in running the retreat.

> **It's difficult to fully participate in the retreat when you are the person running it.**

- You can hire a professional facilitator to run all or part of the retreat. It's difficult to fully participate in the retreat when you are the person running it. See section 6 for more information on hiring a facilitator.

Be sure everyone is clear on who is running the retreat, or specific parts of the retreat. Encourage all members to give that person their full attention and respect. Things run more smoothly when a leader is clearly designated. 🌐

Facilitating the Retreat

Running an Exercise

There is an art to running a retreat exercise successfully. Not every exercise will be a fantastic experience, and not everyone will enjoy the same exercise as much as everyone else. But you can increase the possibility that the exercise will be a valuable experience for all by following a few basic steps.

- Study the exercise – Before you attempt to run an exercise, be sure you have read the materials and thought about how you will run it. How long will you take for each segment? For the entire exercise? Who will go first? What types of discussion do you expect to take place? What challenges do you foresee? Do you need any special materials or props? Is pre-work required?

Facilitating the Retreat, continued

Running an Exercise, continued

- Open the exercise - Introduce the exercise to the Forum, explain the objectives, the process and the expected outcome. Set a warm, comfortable climate where Forum members feel safe embarking on this new experience.

- Run the exercise - Manage the exercise content and processes, manage member participation, set a comfortable pace, and manage transitions. Watch the clock to be sure you're not lagging behind or rushing ahead. Be sure you're including everyone in the exercise.

- Close the exercise - Draw members to conclusion at the appropriate time. This could be the conclusion of the exercise or an intellectual conclusion, depending on the activity.

- Evaluate the outcome - Were the objectives met? Did the members feel it was worthwhile? What unexpected outcomes occurred?

- Follow-up on the exercise - Are there any incomplete aspects of the exercise? Are there any action items to be done? Are there additional, related activities that the group would like to explore as a result of the exercise?

Healthy Deviations from the Group Activity

Part of the facilitator's role is to keep the exercise on track. However, it is natural to veer off onto side tracks sometimes. Be sure you leave ample time on the agenda to allow for a small amount of this. Some of it can be healthy.

Veering off track generally comes in two forms: productive and non-productive. As the facilitator, you must analyze the situation and determine which it is.

- If the activity is non-productive, use re-directive statements to get back on track.

- If the activity is productive, determine if its value is sufficient to sacrifice the agenda and the structure of the current activity. You can either make a judgment call on this yourself, or you can consult with your fellow Forum members for input.

  - If it's not sufficient to disrupt the current activity, put the activity in the 'Parking Lot' for a later time.

  - If it is sufficient to disrupt the current activity, explain to the group that you feel the activity has sufficient merit to move off track temporarily. Set guidelines for the structure and time allocated to the unplanned activity. Proceed as if this is a subset of the current activity and make adjustments to the overall agenda in order to compensate for the lost time.

Facilitating the Retreat, continued

Getting Back on Track with Re-directive Statements

When the group strays off track or a member becomes a challenge, use these statements to help diffuse the situation or shift the meeting focus back on track.

"Let me summarize what I have heard so far, and then let's move on to ... (insert next agenda topic here)."

"I appreciate you sharing your idea. Who else would like to comment?"

"Some of us are actively engaged in the discussion and others are not. What do we need to do to ensure that everyone has an opportunity to offer their ideas?"

"We seem to have gone in a different direction than our agenda. Shall we add this item to our 'Parking Lot' for discussion at a later time?"

"Before we move on to ... (next agenda item), let's summarize the main points of our discussion so far."

"Who would like to add to the comments we just heard?"

"You appear to disagree or have a question. Please tell us what you are thinking."

"Now that we have this idea on the table, let's link it to ... (insert relevant topic or agenda item)" 😊

Seating Chart

Some Forums like to create a seating chart for certain parts of their retreats. This provides the opportunity to seat people together who may not know each other well. It also allows for splitting up people who tend to engage in private conversations or disruptive behaviors.

While a seating chart is not necessary for a retreat, you may want to consider asking people to sit in a different place for different meeting segments. This gets people talking with different people, breaks up potential cliques, and gives people a fresh, new perspective at each session. Another idea is to mix people up at the meals, making sure that cliques don't form between members.

It is especially important for young Forums and new members to have the opportunity for one-on-one interaction with every other person in the Forum. There is a natural tendency for the long-term members to sit together and communicate more with each other. But the retreat is an important time to reach out to new members and help them feel welcome and included.

Another way to mix up the seating at a sit-down dinner is to have people change seats after every course, with every other person moving two seats to the left. It ensures that people have the opportunity to talk with different people throughout the meal. 😊

Action List

A flip chart is a handy tool to have on your retreat. Not only might you need it for some of the exercises, it's a handy way to keep a running Action List and Parking Lot throughout the retreat. By writing items on a flip chart, everyone sees the item, understands its importance, and knows that it won't be forgotten.

Throughout the retreat, keep a running list of follow-up items, action items and decisions. You may also want to keep a parking lot of items that are tabled for discussion at a later time.

Consider assigning responsibility for the Action List as a role during the retreat, as in "Joe, you're responsible for keeping the Action List."

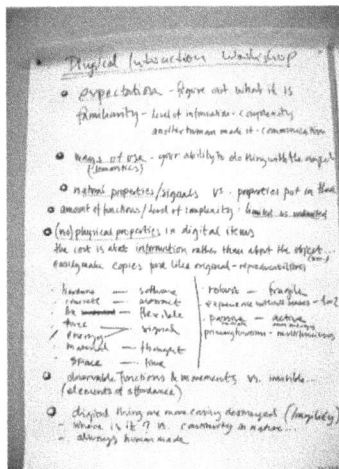

At the end of the retreat, review the list to be sure everyone is in agreement on what happens next and who is responsible for each item. Be realistic about what can be done and in what time frame. Quantify the issues so that the completion can be measured. Vague action items are less likely to get done.

Plan to review the Action List at your Forum meetings (during Housekeeping is a good time to do this) to be sure there is follow-through.

Portable flip charts are available at most office supply stores. Remember to bring flip chart markers for legible viewing. ☺

Minutes of the Meeting

Most Forums do not keep minutes of their retreat due to the confidential nature of the content. However, some Forums track attendance and timeliness throughout the retreat as a matter of process. Also, there may be specific exercises or discussion that would benefit from having notes for reference at a later time. Decide when this is appropriate and assign responsibility for this type of note-taking to a specific person. This person can be the point person later for those who want to follow-up and get copies of the information.

If you do keep minutes of your Forum retreat, be sure that confidential information is not included, or take special precautions to maintain the privacy of the document. Also, remember to remove flip chart papers from your meeting room if you are meeting in a public venue where confidential information could be at risk. ☺

Assigning Retreat Roles

At the beginning of the retreat, assign roles to get everyone involved and supportive working toward the objectives. A list of possible roles is shown here. Feel free to create your own roles to fit your retreat.

- time keeper
- action list keeper
- parking lot keeper
- activities coordinator
- food and beverage coordinator
- process observer
- treasurer

Remember to review the ground rules that were established before the retreat. ☺

Chapter 6
Professional Facilitators

Five Reasons to Hire a Facilitator

Facilitators are a powerful addition to your retreat. There is a cost associated with it, but the help of a skilled facilitator can far outweigh the associated cost. Here are five key reasons why your Forum may want to consider hiring a facilitator.

1. Paid facilitators are experts in their field. These people can help your Forum achieve new levels of depth, introduce new concepts and inject new energy in your Forum. They can also help a Forum that is struggling to identify potential problems, as well as guide the group through conflicts and challenges.

2. Having a facilitator puts all members of the Forum on an even playing field. The moderator and the retreat planners can step back from their leadership roles and be fully present for the retreat exercises. By having a professional facilitator run the retreat, all Forum members can participate as peers and equal members.

3. An outside facilitator alleviates some of the burden of retreat planning. The facilitator is responsible for providing their own content and materials. Depending on whether the facilitator is hired for the entire retreat or a portion of the retreat, this added help can alleviate a significant burden for the retreat planners and the moderator.

4. Bringing in a professional facilitator is a change of pace, especially for Forums that have been together for many years. The new person adds a new dimension and new perspectives to the retreat experience.

5. Using a professional facilitator is a best practice that has been used by Forums for many years. Some Forums bring in a facilitator for every retreat, while other Forums have never used a professional facilitator. The recommended best practice is to hire a retreat facilitator at least once every two years. ☻

What Does a Facilitator Do?

Some facilitators will plan and organize your entire retreat. Others facilitate a specific portion of the retreat. You will need to clarify this, along with your retreat objectives when you are selecting a facilitator.

A good facilitator can be a powerful element toward having a successful retreat. The "external expert" factor brings added focus to the retreat exercises. The facilitator is singularly focused on providing a positive experience for your Forum – that is what they are paid to do.

What Does a Facilitator Do?, continued

A good facilitator will demonstrate the following skills:

- Ability to listen well, without judging and without interjecting their own beliefs.

- Stays neutral about conversations, disagreements and decisions.

- Has ability to assess when the group is stuck, bored, frustrated, or needs a change of pace – and the ability to take corrective action.

- Manages group activities effectively.

- Encourages participation from all members of the Forum.

- Guides the group and/or individual members to address problem behaviors.

- Accepts feedback from the group without being defensive or close-minded.

- Keeps the retreat interesting and well-paced.

Types of Facilitators

Facilitators fall into three main categories:

Forum Experts – a number of facilitators have been certified as Forum trainers, and many have been certified for advanced levels of Forum training. These people understand Forum processes, protocols, structure and content. Some of them are members of organizations like YPO and EO so they may have the added benefit of being in a Forum themselves. If your primary goal is to work on your Forum, a Forum expert is a wise choice. They observe behaviors and interactions, and they can help members understand how they are working together as a group.

Group Facilitators – there are many people who work full-time as professional facilitators, specializing in group dynamics. These people are not necessarily familiar with the Forum concept. It is wise for someone to spend time with this type of facilitator before the retreat to educate them on Forum processes and protocols. Otherwise, you may spend part of your retreat trying to educate them.

Topical Experts – experts abound in a variety of developmental topics. For example, you may want to learn more about motivating employees, or strategic planning, or personal estate planning. You may want to bring in a psychology expert to conduct an assessment on the Forum and walk you through the results. These types of experts are not likely to be involved in the rest of your retreat – only in the time when you are covering their field of expertise. Therefore, you will probably bring this type of expert in for a day or a half-day to work with your Forum on the selected area. You would facilitate the rest of the retreat on your own.

Advantages and Disadvantages of a Hired Facilitator

Advantages:

An external facilitator can be an objective third party to work through Forum issues. The facilitator can be neutral because they have no personal stake in the outcome.

The facilitator handles many of the planning aspects for your retreat, thereby alleviating the burden from the retreat planners.

The facilitator runs most (if not all) of the retreat exercises, thereby taking the burden off of the moderator and other Forum members. Everyone can participate fully in every exercise.

The facilitator adds a new dimension to the retreat– introducing new content and fresh, new ideas.

The facilitator can observe the Forum and identify areas of strength and weakness, then guide the Forum toward improvement.

Disadvantages:

The chemistry the facilitator establishes with the Forum is critical to the success of the retreat. If the chemistry isn't right, some members may shut down or refuse to open up during exercises.

A bad facilitator can result in a bad experience. Be sure you hire an experienced facilitator and be sure to check references. A retreat is a terrible thing to waste!

Facilitators charge for their time and their fee will be added to the cost of the retreat. ☻

Finding a Facilitator

There are several sources for facilitators. First, decide on what type of facilitator you are looking for – a Forum expert, a group facilitator, or a subject matter expert. Refer to your organization's website for a list of certified Forum facilitators. Check out www.forumsherpa.com for more options. For other types of facilitators, you can talk with other Forums for referrals, check with fellow business owners, conduct an online search for specific types of facilitators, or use your own network.

Before engaging a facilitator, be sure you have confidence in his or her skills, knowledge and integrity. Talk with the person one-on-one to get a sense of their personality and style. Check references with other Forums. Are they a good fit for your Forum? What are the goals of your retreat? Is this person equipped to help you achieve your goals? ☻

Retreat Facilitator's Supply Checklist

- flip chart
- set of flip chart markers
- post-it notes
- paper and pens/pencils
- masking tape
- stapler & staple remover
- scissors
- clock or timer

Cost of Facilitators

Many facilitators charge a flat rate for the retreat plus travel expenses. The rate varies based on how much time you ask them to spend with the Forum and how much experience they have. To keep costs in check, be sure to clarify the following in advance:

- Are there extra charges for preparation time, pre-retreat surveys, interviews, etc.?

- Are there charges for travel time or down time?

- Will the facilitator participate in extra-curricular activities?

- Are there extra charges for materials, copying, supplies, etc.?

- Does the facilitator need A/V equipment to conduct exercises?

- Will the facilitator make their own travel arrangements? Has a budget been established for this? (For example, you may want to clarify first-class or coach tickets.)

- Are there extra charges for post-retreat follow-up?

Note that most facilitators charge the same amount for a ½ day session as a full day session because they are likely to lose the entire day regardless. Some facilitators charge by the hour, but be careful – this may include travel time.

Rates are negotiated directly with the facilitator. Rates vary widely, but you can expect to pay somewhere between $2500 and $7500 U.S. per day plus expenses for a retreat facilitator. Get the agreement in writing, and be sure to specify how all the extras will be handled. ☺

Introducing the Facilitator

The facilitator is an important part of your retreat, and it's important to introduce them to your Forum members in advance. Most facilitators are happy to provide you with a bio (professional CV or profile) that you can distribute.

Also, clarify the facilitator's role with the Forum before, during and after the retreat. If there will be a pre-retreat survey or a phone interview, be sure people know to expect this. Explain when these activities will take place and how long they will take.

Clarity on these issues makes the members feel more comfortable about what to expect. It also helps the facilitator to step into their role more easily at the retreat.

On the flip side, provide the facilitator with information about the group: how many members are there, how long have they been together, are there any special issues the Forum is dealing with. Don't let the facilitator be blindsided by problems that you already know about. However, don't go into too much depth or you could create unnecessary biases, especially if the facilitator is only hearing YOUR opinion. It's generally best to simply let the facilitator know that there is an issue, and let them explore the details at the retreat in their own way. ☺

Chapter 7
Common Retreat Challenges

Someone Cancels at the Last Minute

For many Forums, attendance at the annual retreat is mandatory and the Forum norms/constitution states that missing the retreat will result in automatic removal from the Forum. First, let's look at why this is a common practice, and then let's talk about possible alternative resolutions.

There are two key reasons why retreat attendance is mandatory for most Forums. One, attendance at the retreat is a symbol of commitment to the Forum, and aside from catastrophic situations, absence is simply not an option. A significant amount of planning, time and effort go into organizing the retreat. Deposits and reservations have been made that may not be refundable. Some people may have overcome hardships to be able to attend. Therefore, absence may be viewed as a lack of respect for fellow Forum members.

The second reason why retreat attendance is mandatory for most Forums is that the retreat itself is often a catalyst for building depth and reaching new levels in the Forum. The person who misses the retreat isn't part of that experience and therefore, they don't have the same connection, bonding and memories to draw from. This ultimately degrades the impact of the retreat for all the other members. It is unfair and frustrating to those who committed their time and energy to the retreat to lose its impact because of an absent member.

Consult your Forum norms/constitution for your retreat policy and contact the person to be sure they understand the consequences of missing the retreat. Certainly, the reason for cancellation is important, but it may not change the outcome. Talk with other members of the Forum, if necessary, to determine how you will handle the situation. Most importantly, follow the rules as outlined in your Forum norms/constitution.

Listed below are several actual situations where Forums found alternate resolutions:

- One member had a death in the immediate family, the member's father, one day before the retreat. The Forum was able to reschedule the retreat several weeks later.

- One member's child was in a serious car accident two days before the retreat, and was in the hospital in a coma. The retreat couldn't be rescheduled due to reservations and deposits. However, the Forum unanimously voted to excuse the member from the retreat without penalty.

- One member was having severe business problems and due to several recent events, he felt that three days away could result in bankruptcy. The Forum decided to scrap their agenda and spend the entire retreat helping the member with his business problems. The member attended the retreat, and ultimately, the Forum was able to help him save his business. 😬

Someone Needs to Arrive Late or Leave Early

Arriving late and leaving early are extremely disruptive to the retreat and should be avoided at all costs. Many Forums have increased fines for this, and some Forums consider it as serious as missing the retreat.

If someone MUST arrive late, you might consider delaying the start time for everyone and extending the retreat on the back end. Conversely, if someone MUST leave early, consider moving up the start time so that everyone can spend the full retreat time together. If these options are not feasible, refer to your Forum norms/constitution on how to handle the situation. ☺

Someone Doesn't Do Their Pre-Work

First, attempt to avert this problem before it happens by sending frequent reminders about the pre-work before the retreat. It is frustrating to those who have completed the pre-work to wait on those who haven't. It also disrupts the agenda, especially on exercises that require considerable time and introspective thought. Some exercises require that people bring physical items with them to the retreat, and it then becomes impossible to complete these exercises. This is inconsiderate and unfair to the rest of the Forum.

When you realize that some people have not completed their pre-work, immediately engage in a discussion with the Forum on how to handle the situation. Does the agenda need to be adjusted? Should the retreat be paused while the laggards catch up? What should the rest of the Forum do while they're waiting? ☺

Someone Is Overly Quiet or Doesn't Participate

For a person who is exhibiting unusually quiet behavior there could be several possible causes. They may be frustrated with events or people at the retreat. They may be distracted by problems outside of the retreat, such as family issues or problems at work. They may not be feeling well. When you notice these types of behavior, it is usually best to have a private conversation with the person, tell them you've noticed their withdrawal from the group, and ask them how you can help. If possible, share the situation with the entire group afterwards so that everyone understands what it happening. If you noticed the problem, they probably noticed it too, and they may all be able to help if they're aware of the situation.

If the person is upset about the retreat itself, you may want to consider an open discussion about their concerns with the entire group. If the person isn't feeling well, consider adjusting the retreat agenda to give the person time to rest. If the person feels a conflict with another Forum member, determine if it needs to be handled immediately or if it should be postponed for later discussion. If the person has other problems outside of the Forum and unrelated to the retreat, consider adjusting the agenda to give the person time to share the problem. You may even want to schedule an emergency presentation to let the person share the issue in more depth.

Note that some people are naturally quiet and their behavior does not necessarily indicate that anything is wrong. In general, you want to have equal participation from all members of the Forum, so you may want to ask the quiet person for their thoughts periodically. Draw quieter members into the conversations as much as possible and try to balance the input from everyone.

Another tactic to use when it's important for everyone to have input is to have people pair up and discuss the issue. Then have each pair report back to the group. The quiet person may feel more comfortable talking to just one person and letting someone else be the spokesperson for their thoughts. ☺

A Few People Dominate the Discussions

When people are unusually talkative or overbearing, there can be many reasons. Some people have a natural need for attention while others may genuinely want to share their thoughts or expertise. Some people may try to drown out opposing opinions while others may be truly passionate about the topic. Regardless of the cause, it is important to have equal participation and input from everyone. Try to bring others into the conversation, saying something like "We really need to hear from everyone on this. Sarah, could you please share your thoughts with us?" If you still can't balance the conversation, have a private conversation with the offender(s) on break. You can politely ask them if they're aware that they're dominating the conversation and ask if they are willing to try to listen more and talk less.

Another technique is to ask people to speak in turn, going around the Forum in a circle. A more extreme tactic is to ask someone to keep a time log of how long each person talks. After an hour, ask the timekeeper to read back the totals on the time log. This helps to spotlight the people who are dominating the conversation.

As a group, you can discuss the need for balance in conversations. Remind the group of the ground rules which should include something about equal participation and listening well. ☺

The Group Keeps Wandering Off Track

Retreat exercises can get off track for a variety of reasons. Perhaps people are genuinely more interested in a side conversation; perhaps people want to avoid a particular topic, or perhaps people are simply bored. Getting too far off track for too long can jeopardize the agenda so it's important to watch the clock and take corrective action when needed.

First you must determine if the off-track discussion is productive or non-productive. If it's non-productive, you can shut it down quickly and move on. However, if it's productive you must then decide if the unplanned discussion is more important than the planned discussion. This can be a group decision whereby you simply ask the Forum members if they're comfortable continuing on the new track with the understanding that the original track will have to be delayed or abandoned.

As the moderator, you must continually assess the agenda, the time and the importance of each discussion. Assign a time keeper to help you watch the time, and a process observer to watch the conversations. These people can help you with the job of keeping the group on track. ☺

There Isn't Enough Time for the Exercises

Careful planning of the agenda can minimize time problems, but even the best planned agenda can have design flaws. There is a fine line between having too much or too little on the agenda. Too much results in feeling rushed. Exercises may be ineffective, and some activities may have to be skipped. Too little on the agenda can result in boredom. People may not feel they're getting enough value from the retreat. They are wasting their time. It's more common to have too much on the agenda rather than too little, and if you must err, it's generally better to err on this side. It's easier to cut out exercises than to add in new ones.

The exercises in this book provide estimated times for all exercises, assuming a Forum of eight people. When planning the agenda, remember to allow "white space" – this is open time for people to talk and relax between planned activities. This is an important part of the retreat where social interaction takes place and interpersonal relationships develop.

There Isn't Enough Time for the Exercises, continued

If you still have problems with running out of time, first determine if the exercises are being run efficiently. Are you timing the discussions? Are some people rambling or dominating the conversation? If you get too far behind, have a candid discussion with the Forum about how to adjust the agenda and get back on track. Can we skip one of the exercises? Do we need to work through lunch? Attempt to get back on the planned timeline as soon as possible. ☺

Someone Violates the Ground Rules

The established ground rules for your retreat have little meaning unless they are observed in practice. It's important that everyone adheres to the ground rules – including the moderator / facilitator. When the rules are broken, remind people of their commitment to the ground rules. Depending on the infraction, you may want to do this as a group, or you may want to take a break and talk with the person one-on-one.

It's a good idea to remind everyone of the ground rules at the beginning of the retreat. You may want to write them on a flip chart and tape it on the wall as a continuous reminder. ☺

An Intense Conflict Breaks Out

Conflicts are uncomfortable for most people, especially intense ones. Conflicts can break out for a variety of reasons, for example:

- someone feels threatened, embarrassed or exposed

- someone feels left out, ignored or under-valued

- someone feels pressure to support something they don't agree with

- someone is dealing with a personal, unrelated issue that is causing them to feel severe stress

Conflict resolution skills become critically important if this happens during the retreat. If two people are in extreme conflict with each other, the moderator may need to pause the meeting for a break and encourage the two people to work out the issue on their own if possible (without an audience). If this isn't possible, the moderator can join the conversation to act as an independent third party. Finally, if the conflict still can't be resolved, the issue can be brought to the entire Forum.

A powerful method of working through an emotionally charged issue is to ask people to divide the issue into four components: Facts, Opinions, Feelings and Wants. You can literally take four sheets of flip chart paper and write each of the four words at the top of each sheet of paper. Then give everyone the opportunity to express their thoughts in each of the four categories. After everyone has had the opportunity to share their thoughts, ask for suggestions on how to resolve the issue. Work toward consensus, always listening carefully and being cautious not to be judgmental of anyone's feelings. Refer to the Forum Conflict Resolution Guide (www.forumsherpa.com) for more information on handling conflict.

Another technique is to ask each person to restate the opposing party's view. This ensures that each party is truly listening to the other person's perspective.

An Intense Conflict Breaks Out, continued

Finally, remember that conflict can be a positive catalyst for change. It can result in clarification of important issues and resolution of interpersonal conflicts. It can inspire authentic communication and help release pent-up emotion. In many cases, it enhances people's understanding of each other. Often times, people feel better and closer after the conflict is resolved. It can be a breakthrough for some people and for the entire Forum. 😎

Someone Becomes Emotional and Breaks Into Tears

Emotions are more likely to be displayed at a retreat than in traditional Forum meetings. People are away from their usual, professional environment and in a more relaxed setting. There is a feeling of camaraderie and safety with the Forum. Getting away from traditional boundaries can bring emotions to the surface.

Often the person who experiences an intense emotional outburst is as surprised as everyone else. Know that they may feel embarrassed and uncomfortable. How the other Forum members react to their tears is an important part of how people will feel about being open in the future. For example, if someone were to make a joke or make light of the situation, this could not only further embarrass the distressed person, but others learn that it's not safe to show their emotions with the Forum.

Each situation will be different and should be handled according to the person, the level of intensity and the surrounding circumstances. Always be considerate of the person's feelings. Give them time to continue if they want – perhaps they need to "get it all out." In addition to offering compassion, it can be helpful to offer the person a tissue or a glass of water. This provides physical comfort and it offers a momentary diversion from the intensity of the situation. A pat on the back or a hug can also provide comfort. If the person continues to have difficulty composing themselves, you might ask them if they'd like to take a break. Take your cues from the person in distress. Try to think of how you would want to be treated if you were in their shoes and treat them the same way. 😎

A Retreat Exercise Does Not Go Well

Great exercises can be poorly executed, and not all exercises are great exercises. Sometimes after an exercise, the Forum may feel unsatisfied – they may even feel they have wasted their time. Be aware that this will happen on occasion. It doesn't mean the entire retreat is ruined, it's just a temporary setback.

Before you move on, it's useful to debrief on what went wrong. Not only does this let people vent their frustration a bit, it can provide insight into the root of the problem. This is particularly important if the problem is something that can be corrected on future exercises. But don't dissect it too long – that can become even more frustrating. It's over. After a short debriefing, it's time to move on to more productive things. 😎

Chapter 8
Wrapping Up the Retreat

Closing the Retreat

As your retreat draws to a close, it's important to bring the event to a comfortable conclusion. Retreats are an emotionally intense experience for many people, and they will appreciate the time to reflect on what has happened. A rushed closing can undermine some of the progress made by the group over the course of the retreat.

The retreat close is an ideal opportunity to debrief and review the retreat's effectiveness. It's also the right time to be sure the next steps are clear and you have a plan for implementing group decisions. Don't let your progress go to waste!

Here are a few steps to include in your retreat closing:

- Thank everyone for participating. Thank the retreat planners for their work. Thank the moderator and/or facilitator for running the exercises. Thank everyone for their time, effort and creativity.

- Review the action list you made during the retreat. These items should have been scribed on a flip chart throughout the retreat and now is the time to be sure everyone has clarity on who is responsible for taking action after the retreat. Ideally, people should volunteer to take responsibility of their action items. People are more likely to complete the task if it's their choice to do it. Forcing a task on someone who doesn't want to do it is often a recipe for failure.

- Review the decisions you made and be sure you know who is responsible for taking any necessary actions and when they should take place. Update your Forum norms/constitution if necessary to reflect the decisions.

- Complete a retreat evaluation form. Samples are provided on the following pages. Give people time to complete the form and collect them on the spot, if possible..

- Use a closing exercise to inspire a positive, final closure for the retreat. Several exercises are included in Part 2 of this book. 😊

Retreat Evaluation

A retreat evaluation is an invaluable tool for closing your retreat. It affords the Forum several benefits:

- It gives the Forum an honest view of whether expectations were met.

- It may clear the air on some issues.

- It will be helpful next year for planning the next retreat.

Ideally, the retreat evaluation should be done at the very end of the retreat, before the retreat officially closes and everyone leaves to go their own way. Capturing people's thoughts and ideas while they're still fresh is generally more effective than waiting for your next meeting. Also, at the end of a retreat, people are more in the Forum mindset and, therefore, they are more interested in providing input.

Two sample retreat evaluation forms are provided here. The first is more quantitative and the second is more qualitative. Choose the one that is more appropriate for your Forum, or make up your own with information from both survey examples. ☺

Post-Retreat Survey #1

Surveys are a way for us to assess retreat performance and effectiveness. Your response will help us plan next year's retreat to be an even better experience. This will take less than 5 minutes! Do it now!

Please rate your retreat experience on each of the following (1=Lousy and 10= Excellent).

	Lousy									Excellent
	1	**2**	**3**	**4**	**5**	**6**	**7**	**8**	**9**	**10**
Retreat planning process										
Pre-preparation of participants										
Attendance of entire group										
Punctuality of members at sessions										
Knowledge of other members										
Experience sharing of other members										
Work exercises – depth & diversity										
Fun activities										
Relaxation and social time										
Openness of the Forum										
Development of trust										
Moderator – leadership										
Facilitator (if applicable)										
Retreat location										
Retreat take away value										
Achievement of retreat objectives										

Comments:

Please share anything else you like. Comments, complaints, suggestions and ideas are welcome!

_____

_____

_____

Post-Retreat Survey #2

1) What three things did you like most about the retreat?

2) What three things could be changed to improve the next retreat?

3) In your opinion, the length of the retreat was... (check one)

    _____   too short

    _____   about right

    _____   too long

4) Please rate each retreat exercise on a scale of 1 to 10 (1 is not helpful, 10 is very valuable):

    Exercise #1 (insert title):   1   2   3   4   5   6   7   8   9   10

    Exercise #2 (insert title):   1   2   3   4   5   6   7   8   9   10

    Exercise #3 (insert title):   1   2   3   4   5   6   7   8   9   10

    Exercise #4 (insert title):   1   2   3   4   5   6   7   8   9   10

    Exercise #5 (insert title):   1   2   3   4   5   6   7   8   9   10

    Exercise #6 (insert title):   1   2   3   4   5   6   7   8   9   10

    Exercise #7 (insert title):   1   2   3   4   5   6   7   8   9   10

5) Do you have any comments on specific exercises?

Post-Retreat Survey #2, continued

6) What exercises/activities would you like to see on the next retreat?

7) Do you feel the retreat goals were met? Provide your answer on a scale of 1 to 10.

8) Please provide comments about how retreat goals were met for you or why they were not.

Collect the evaluations and compile them before your next Forum meeting. (Alternatively, use an online survey tool to collect feedback anonymously and compile it automatically.) During the next meeting, ask the moderator to allot time on the agenda for a short debrief on the retreat. Fifteen minutes should be plenty of time. Discuss the results and talk about any issues that came up. Make notes of any changes the Forum would like to make on next year's retreat.

Finally, save the evaluations for your retreat next year. Your trip planners next year will thank you for it! ☺

Using Retreat Outcomes for Ongoing Forum Improvement

Remember to keep the process alive. Typically, there is an upswing in morale and commitment after the retreat. Provide a continuous feedback loop after the retreat to capitalize on these benefits. For example, the moderator could ask for periodic reports on action items.

Physical reminders are also helpful. Share pictures from the retreat with each other. Or select a favorite picture of the entire group, blow it up, frame it and give copies to every Forum member. A decorative object, such as a paperweight from the retreat location, sitting on someone's desk can serve as a reminder of the spirit of the retreat.

Also, consider holding a mini-retreat midyear to re-energize. Refer to Section 4, Sample Agenda, 1-Night Retreat (Mini-Retreat) for more information.

A successful retreat can be a peak experience for everyone in the Forum. Acknowledge the progress made and the accomplishments achieved. Celebrate ongoing milestones as they occur. Keep the momentum alive and the impact of the retreat can last long beyond the few days you spend together. ☺

Category 1

Retreat Openers

Use these exercises at the beginning of the retreat to set the tone, the expectations and the ground rules for the entire retreat.

Refer to Part 1 of this book, Planning Your Retreat, for information on how to facilitate exercises. Time estimates for individual exercises are based on an 8-person Forum. Adjust the time estimates as needed to accommodate the size of your Forum.

Category 1 Exercises

forumsherpa

Retreat Visualization

Retreat Visualization is an exercise that enables Forum members to contemplate their expectations for the retreat by envisioning their mindset at the end of the retreat. (As Steven Covey says, "Begin with the end in mind.") Members gain clarity on what they want to get out of the retreat, and at the same time, they learn what others are expecting.

Objectives

- To clarify individual objectives and expectations
- To compile and share group objectives
- To build enthusiasm for the retreat

Facilitator Info

Depth Level:	Light
Facilitation Skills:	Basic
Estimated Time:	30 minutes
Tools Needed:	None
Handouts:	Retreat Visualization Worksheet
Pre-work:	Complete the Retreat Visualization Worksheet in advance. If people attempt to answer the questions spontaneously, you may begin to get "group think" and you'll generate fewer ideas. Approximately 20 minutes.
Notes:	Start with a different person for each question. If you start with the same person every time, their thoughts can begin to dominate the exercise.
Author/Source:	Unknown, adapted for Forum

Facilitator Instructions

1) At the beginning of the retreat, go around the room and ask each person to share their answer to the first question.
2) Then, move to the second question and ask each person to share their answer.
3) Continue this process until everyone has shared their answer to all seven questions.

Retreat Visualization Worksheet

Imagine that it's already the end of the retreat. It's Sunday evening and this is the first chance you've had to take a moment and reflect back on the retreat. You're still amazed at what an incredible success it was, and how much you got out of it. You decide to sit back for a few moments and savor your experiences and review how it came to be the success that it was. As you think about the weekend, many of the specific details come back to you.

Answer the following questions:

1.   What were the high points of the retreat for you?

2.   What things contributed to the success of the retreat?

3.   What things did you do during the retreat to create such a satisfying experience?

4.   What was the moment where you were having the most fun?

5.   What was the most challenging part of the retreat for you?

6.   You remember being really surprised by something that happened during the retreat. What was it?

7.   Looking back on the retreat, it's clear to you that the most valuable thing you took away from the weekend was:

Print this form, answer the questions and bring it with you to the retreat. We will begin our retreat by discussing expectations for the weekend. We'll use your answers to help create a list of expectations and we'll check our success at the end of the retreat.

Great Expectations

Great Expectations is an exercise that prompts Forum members to think about their expectations and objectives for the retreat. Members gain clarity on what they want to get out of the retreat, and at the same time, they learn what others are expecting.

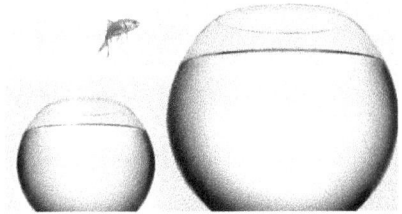

Objectives

- To clarify individual expectations of the retreat
- To compile and share group objectives
- To build enthusiasm for the retreat

Facilitator Info

Depth Level:	Light
Facilitation Skills:	Basic
Estimated Time:	15 minutes
Tools Needed:	Flipchart, markers
Handouts:	None
Pre-work:	None
Notes:	• Optionally, ask each person to write their name after their expectation. • If there are conflicting expectations, engage in a discussion on how to resolve the differing viewpoints.
Author/Source:	Ellie Byrd

Facilitator Instructions

1) One at a time, ask each person to write one of their expectations for the retreat on a flipchart. (Fun ones are okay!)
2) Have the person pass the marker to the next person and let them come up and write one of their expectations.
3) Keep going around the room until you run out of expectations. This may take two or three times around the room.
4) Post the flipchart on the wall somewhere in plain view for the entire retreat.
5) Note that you may want to take a pulse check once or twice during the retreat to see if people are happy with how the retreat is progressing. Is the pace okay? Are we staying on track? Are people pleased about how the retreat is going? Are there any adjustments we should make?
6) At the end of the retreat, go back to the flipchart and see how many of the expectations were met.

Expectations & Outcomes

Expectations & Outcomes is an exercise that asks each Forum member to write private notes about what they expect to get out of the retreat, then review their notes at the end of the retreat for comparison. Members reflect on whether their expectations were met and whether their perceptions have changed during the retreat.

Objectives

- To begin the retreat by having Forum members think about what they would like to get out of the retreat
- To end the retreat by reflection on how well their expectations were met

Facilitator Info

Depth Level:	Light
Facilitation Skills:	Basic
Estimated Time:	10 minutes at beginning of retreat 10 minutes at end of retreat
Tools Needed:	3 x 5 cards, pens/pencils and envelopes for each person, flipchart, markers
Handouts:	None
Pre-work:	None
Notes:	Optionally, you could ask people to share their expectations at the beginning of the retreat, then discuss how well their expectations were met at the end of the retreat. This variation, however, may alter what people write on their card.
Author/Source:	"Retreats That Work", adapted for Forum

Facilitator Instructions, Part One

Part one occurs at the beginning of the retreat.

1) On the flipchart, write down the following three questions.
   a) The main thing I would like to get out of this retreat is...
   b) One thing I am concerned about is...
   c) One thing I would like to learn during this retreat is...
2) Give a 3 x 5 card to each person.
3) Ask them to answer these three questions on their card. Tell them to be completely honest and write down the first thing that comes to mind. Nobody will see their card but them.
4) Give everyone about five minutes to answer the three questions.
5) Give each person an envelope. Ask them to put their card inside the envelope, seal it and write their name on the outside.
6) Collect the envelopes until the end of the retreat when you will return the envelopes.

Expectations & Outcomes, continued

Facilitator Instructions, Part Two

Part two occurs at the end of the retreat.

1) At the end of the retreat, give everyone their envelope back.
2) Have everyone open their envelope and read their thoughts.
3) Ask them to reflect on whether their expectations were met. Also, consider how their perspective may have changed from the beginning of the retreat until the end.
4) Ask for volunteers who would like to share their insights.

Ground Rules

Ground Rules is an exercise that establishes a clear understanding of behaviors, rules and agreements that are to be followed on the retreat. Having clarity on ground rules can help the Forum to avoid uncomfortable situations, disagreements and conflicts.

Objectives

- To formulate ground rules that everyone agrees upon
- To learn from past experiences – especially the bad ones

Facilitator Info

Depth Level:	Light
Facilitation Skills:	Basic
Estimated Time:	20 minutes
Tools Needed:	Flipchart, markers, paper & pens/pencils
Handouts:	None
Pre-work:	None
Notes:	Examples of ground rules topics include: cell phone usage, break times, alcohol consumption, side bar conversations, etc.
Author/Source:	Unknown, adapted for Forum

Facilitator Instructions

1) Briefly lead a discussion on how we can learn from bad experiences. They become a benefit when we use them to avoid repeating the bad experience.
2) Ask each person to write down a bad experience from a previous retreat or meeting. This may include things that they personally said or did and regretted later, or situations that caused conflict.
3) Take turns asking each person to share their bad experience. Try to avoid using names when telling stories. Write a short phrase on the flipchart that describes the experience.
4) Some people may have more than one bad experience to share.
5) After everyone has shared their bad experiences, you will have a list of behaviors and problems that the group will probably want to avoid. Now, start a new flipchart page that establishes a ground rule to avoid each of the bad experiences. Let others help you develop the ground rules and scribe them on the flipchart.
6) At the end of the exercise, ask if everyone is willing to commit to following these ground rules.
7) Post the ground rules somewhere in plain sight for the entire retreat.

How Are We Doing?

How Are We Doing is an exercise that helps meetings run more smoothly. Members have the opportunity to express their viewpoints in a non-threatening manner and everyone becomes more involved in the success of the meeting.

Objectives

- To provide a temperature check on how the meeting is progressing
- To raise awareness about common behaviors that can derail a meeting
- To enable Forum members to have a fun, safe outlet for expressing their feelings during the retreat

Facilitator Info

Depth Level:	Light
Facilitation Skills:	Basic
Estimated Time:	5-minute discussion, then available throughout the meeting as needed
Tools Needed:	One set of animal cards per person
Handouts:	None
Pre-work:	None
Notes:	<ul><li>This exercise is useful in newer Forums where people may not yet feel comfortable voicing their opinions.</li><li>Create your own cards with animals that depict specific behaviors that your Forum may need to address.</li><li>The cards are intended to be a fun, light-hearted way to address challenging issues and behaviors. They may NOT be appropriate in every situation.</li><li>You can use these cards to gauge the progress of the meeting. For example, if you'd like to know whether the current discussion should continue, you can ask everyone to hold up the Dead Horse card if they want to move on. This gives you a consensus on whether to continue the current discussion or move on to the next topic.</li></ul>
Author/Source:	Unknown, adapted for Forum

Facilitator Instructions

1) There are a number of behaviors and situations that can cause problems on the retreat. Explain that the cards are a way of enabling members to identify these behaviors and situations in a fun, non-threatening manner.
2) Use the Dead Horse card as an example. The Dead Horse card may be pulled out and placed in the middle of the table by anyone who feels the discussion has reached the end of its usefulness. In other words, the activity is done, the horse is dead. Let's move on to something else.

How Are We Doing?, continued

3) Describe each of the cards in the envelope and then hand out the envelopes to everyone. The examples provided below are:

   a) Turtle – the activity is starting late, or someone is late to the meeting.
   b) Dead Horse – the activity is done, let's move on.
   c) Monkey – someone is being overly silly, cracking too many jokes, not paying attention, etc.
   d) Parrot – someone is overly talkative, talking too much, interrupting people, etc.
   e) Fox – someone is being dishonest, or not opening up enough.

Running Late	Moving Too Slow
Acting Silly	**Talking Too Much**
Acting guarded, sneaky or dishonest	(Create your own)

Balloon Time Keeping

Balloon Time Keeping is a lighthearted way of raising awareness on the importance of time-keeping throughout the retreat. Everyone has the opportunity to participate which gets members more involved in the success of the retreat.

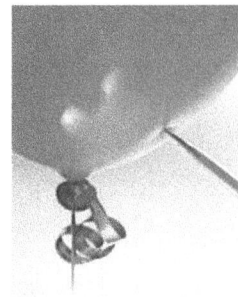

Objectives

- To raise awareness about staying on time
- To enable Forum members to have a safe, light-hearted method for letting someone know they're talking too long or the meeting is dragging

Facilitator Info

Depth Level:	Light
Facilitation Skills:	Basic
Estimated Time:	3-minute discussion, then available throughout the meeting as needed
Tools Needed:	A bag of balloons, ball of string to tie the balloons to chairs, scissors, one closed safety pin for each person.
Handouts:	None
Pre-work:	Blow up the balloons and tie several of them to the back of each person's chair.
Notes:	<ul><li>This exercise can be particularly useful in Forums where timeliness is a problem. It can also be helpful if members have a tendency to ramble.</li><li>You can make a competition out of blowing up the balloons by splitting into two groups and seeing which group can blow up the most balloons in five minutes.</li></ul>
Author/Source:	Unknown, adapted for Forum

Facilitator Instructions

1) Have a brief discussion on the importance of staying on time throughout the retreat.
2) Anyone can pop a balloon if someone is talking too long, or if the allotted time for a particular activity has been reached. The "pop" not only startles the ears, it serves as a funny reminder for everyone to stay on time.

Category 2

Ice Breakers

Use these exercises early in the retreat (or each morning) to loosen up, lighten up, and have fun.

Refer to Part 1 of this book, Planning Your Retreat, for information on how to facilitate exercises. Time estimates for individual exercises are based on an 8-person Forum. Adjust the time estimates as needed to accommodate the size of your Forum.

Category 2 Exercises

forumsherpa

Guess the Lie

Guess the Lie is a fun exercise that helps people get to know each other better by learning fun facts about each other.

Objectives

- To learn more about each other
- To loosen up, laugh, and have fun

Facilitator Info

Depth Level:	Light
Facilitation Skills:	Basic
Estimated Time:	15 minutes
Tools Needed:	None
Handouts:	None
Pre-work:	None
Notes:	• This exercise is also called "Two Truths and a Lie." • This exercise can be repeated anytime. Everyone has plenty of obscure facts (and fictions!) they can share with the Forum.
Author/Source:	Unknown, adapted for Forum

Facilitator Instructions

1. Explain the purpose of the exercise and ask each person to think of three statements about themselves – two that are true and one that is false. All three statements should be things that nobody in the Forum knows about them. Here are some examples:
   a) I flunked high school chemistry.
   b) My aunt was an Olympic bronze medalist in free-style swimming.
   c) I've had more than 25 speeding tickets.
   d) I accidentally scored a basket for the wrong team in high school when I got confused about which side of the court I was on.
   e) I'm terrified of spiders.
2. Give people several minutes to think of their statements.
3. Go around the room, one person at a time, and ask each person say their three statements – two true and one false.
   a) Let the Forum discuss which one they think is false, and attempt to achieve consensus.
   b) Only allow one or two minutes of discussion on each person's statements. Note that consensus may be impossible.
   c) After everyone has guessed which statement they think is false, let the person reveal their lie.
4. Then, continue to the next person and repeat.

That's Incredible!

That's Incredible is an exercise that helps Forum members learn fun facts about each other. People learn how well they know each other and how much they don't know about each other!

Objectives

- To disseminate pre-conceived notions about other participants
- To loosen up, laugh, and have fun
- To learn more about each other

Facilitator Info

Depth Level:	Light
Facilitation Skills:	Basic
Estimated Time:	20 minutes
Tools Needed:	Flipchart, markers, prizes (optional)
Handouts:	Participant's Guess Sheet
Pre-work:	Send an email or text to each participant requesting they reply with an "incredible" secret about themselves. See Email / Text* below.
Notes:	Optionally, at the end of the exercise give a prize to the person who guessed the most correct answers and give another prize to the person who fooled the most people.
Author/Source:	Ellie Byrd

Pre-Work

1) Send an email or text to each participant with the following information at least one week before the retreat:

---

*Email / Text:

1) Think of something about yourself that you're ABSOLUTELY sure no one else in the Forum knows about you. This should be something lighthearted – perhaps something quirky, or funny, or amazing. Here are some examples:

- broke my big toe on my wedding day
- accidentally closed my cat in the freezer all night (and it lived!)
- spent the night in jail
- won the talent competition in 3rd grade
- sat next to Billy Joel on an airplane
- shot a hole in my kitchen floor with a 357 Magnum
- owned 26 cars in the last 22 years

2) Send your "incredible" secret back to me. We will use this as a fun ice breaker on the retreat to guess each other's secrets!

That's Incredible!, continued

Pre-Work, continued

2) Compile all of the responses onto a single Guess Sheet. Number the responses but do NOT list the names.
3) Make copies of the Guess Sheet for each participant.

Facilitator Instructions – At the Retreat

1) Explain the objective of the exercise and walk through the process.
2) Distribute the Guess Sheets containing all the "secrets" and ask each participant to guess who turned in each response. Give them five minutes to do this.
3) On a flipchart, list each Forum member's name.
4) Go through each question and let the participants discuss who they think turned in the response. Allow for some healthy laughing and talking, but generally you'll want to identify the author within one minute so that the process doesn't drag on.
5) When the author is identified, ask how many people guessed the person correctly. Write the number next to the person's name on the flipchart.
6) After you have identified all the authors, ask each participant to total the number of correct guesses.
7) Award prizes to the person with the most correct guesses and the person who fooled the most people.

That's Incredible!

Participant's Guess Sheet

The following list was compiled from the "secrets" that everyone sent in. Try to guess which of your fellow Forum members belongs with each secret.

Incredible secret	Guess who	Correct? Yes or No
1. <add a secret here>		
2. <add a secret here>		
3. <add a secret here>		
4. <add a secret here>		
5. <add a secret here>		
6. <add a secret here>		
7. <add a secret here>		
8. <add a secret here>		
9. <add a secret here>		
10. <add a secret here>		

How many correct guesses did you make? _____

How many people did you fool with your secret? _____

The Pig Test

The Pig Test is an exercise that generally sparks laughter and fun. The premise is that the way you draw a picture of a pig is an indication of your personality and preferences. People's drawing skills come into play and a humorous, non-scientific assessment of the drawings follows.

Objectives

- To loosen up, laugh, and have fun
- To learn about personality traits of yourself and others (maybe)

Facilitator Info

Depth Level:	Light
Facilitation Skills:	Basic
Estimated Time:	15 minutes
Tools Needed:	Blank sheets of paper (8 ½ x 11), pencils
Handouts:	None
Pre-work:	None
Notes:	The test is not scientifically proven, but it is a well-known ice breaker tool, freely available at several sites on the internet. Note that this is NOT a validated assessment – it's for fun!
Author/Source:	Unknown, adapted for Forum

Facilitator Instructions

1) Provide each person with a full size, blank sheet of paper for drawing.
2) Ask everyone to draw a pig on their sheet of paper. Explain that artistry skills are not important. This should take about two minutes.
3) Read the Personality Analysis (next page) based on how they drew their pig.
4) Ask for comments on how accurate the analysis was.

The Pig Test, continued

Personality Analysis

If the pig is drawn:

- Toward the top of the page, you are positive and optimistic.
- Toward the middle of the page, you are down to earth, a realist.
- Toward the bottom of the page, you are pessimistic and have a tendency to be negative.

- Facing left, you believe in tradition, are friendly, and remember dates (birthdays, etc.).
- Facing right, you are innovative and active, but you don't have a strong sense of family, nor do you remember dates.
- Facing front (looking at you), you are direct, you enjoy playing devil's advocate, and you neither fear nor avoid directions.

- With many details, you are analytical, cautious and you may tend to be skeptical.
- With few details, you are emotional and sometimes blunt, you care little for details and you are a risk-taker.

- With fewer than 4 legs showing, you are insecure or you are living through a period of major change.
- With 4 legs showing, you are secure, stubborn, and stick to your ideals.

- The size of the ears indicates how good a listener you are. The bigger the better.
- The length of the tail indicates the quality of your sex life!!!! (and again – more is better!)

- With spots on the pig – you are artistic and you have a good sense of humor.
- Without spots on the pig – you prefer simplicity.

Baby Face

Baby Face is a game of guessing who is whom from baby pictures.

Objective

- To have fun

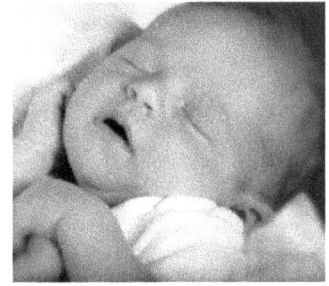

Facilitator Info

Depth Level:	Light
Facilitation Skills:	Basic
Estimated Time:	5 minutes
Tools Needed:	Poster board, glue stick, pens/pencils and paper
Handouts:	None
Pre-work:	Each person must bring a baby picture of themselves to the retreat.
Notes:	None
Author/Source:	Ellie Byrd

Facilitator Instructions

1) Collect the baby pictures before the retreat and position them on a poster board. Number each picture. (Be careful not to damage the pictures!)
2) For fun, you can leave the poster board up throughout the retreat so that people can continue looking at the board and working on their guesses.
3) At the end of the retreat, give everyone a piece of paper and ask them to guess who belongs to each baby picture.
4) At the designated time, ask each person to reveal which picture is theirs. Consider giving a prize to the person who has the most correct guesses, and the person who fools the most people.

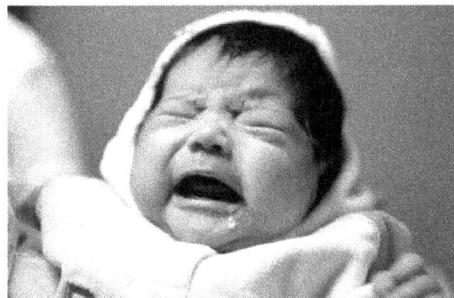

Similarities and Differences

Similarities and Differences is an exercise that helps Forum members learn more about each other – what they have in common and what they don't. It a light, interactive exercise that gets people talking about themselves in a comfortable, fun format.

Objectives

- To look introspectively at your interests and preferences
- To learn new things about your fellow Forum members
- To begin conversations about a wide variety of topics

Facilitator Info

Depth Level:	Light
Facilitation Skills:	Basic
Estimated Time:	20 minutes
Tools Needed:	Pens/pencils
Handouts:	Copies of the Similarities and Differences Worksheet (next page)
Pre-work:	None
Notes:	None
Author/Source:	Jorge Cherbosque

Facilitator Instructions

1) Ask everyone to complete the Similarities and Differences Worksheet by writing their answers in the "My Answer" column.
2) Next, ask participants to see if they can find someone who has the same answer as theirs. Write their name in the "My Match" column.
3) Have everyone rotate and talk with everyone else until they run out of time.
4) How many matches did you get?

Similarities & Differences Worksheet

Question	My Answer	My Match
The most romantic movie I ever saw was:		
My favorite color is:		
One thing that brings me pleasure is:		
The thing that sends me over the edge is:		
The place in the world that brings me the most peace is:		
One thing that makes me feel fearful is:		
Regarding food, I salivate when:		
The spice that best describes my life is:		
If I could be someone else in addition to myself, I would be:		
A culture (not mine) that fascinates me is:		
My favorite musician or group is:		
One word that describes how I feel now is:		
If I could come back in a different profession, I would be:		
One thing that fills my life is:		
The thing I like best about myself is:		

The Name Game

The Name Game is an exercise that helps people learn more about the origin and significance of people's names – first, middle and last. Each person answers a series of questions about their name and shares relevant stories.

Objective

- To learn more about members' backgrounds as it relates to their name

Facilitator Info

Depth Level:	Light
Facilitation Skills:	Basic
Estimated Time:	15 minutes
Tools Needed:	None
Handouts:	None
Pre-work:	None
Notes:	This is a light exercise, good for a fairly new Forum.
Author/Source:	Ellie Byrd

Facilitator Instructions

1) Ask each member to answer the following questions about their name:
   a. State your first, middle, and last name
   b. Give a short history of your name
   c. Who were you named after?
   d. How do you feel about your name?
   e. What nicknames did you have or do you have? How do you feel about these?
   f. Feel free to share any other odd or interesting information about your name
2) Allow for a bit of Q&A after each person shares their information.
3) After everyone has talked about their name, discuss the debriefing questions below.

Debrief Questions

a) How important is a person's name?
b) Can a name cause biases?
c) Did you learn anything surprising about your fellow Forum members during this exercise?

Who Am I?

Who Am I? is a detective game where each person is randomly assigned the name of a famous person or character, then tasked with discovering whose name they've been assigned. Participants must think analytically and interact with each other in a unique and often amusing way to discover who they are.

Objectives

- To loosen up, have fun
- To think analytically
- To get everyone involved
- To encourage participants to develop good questioning and data-gathering/detective skills

Facilitator Info

Depth Level:	Light
Facilitation Skills:	Basic
Estimated Time:	15 minutes
Tools Needed:	Character name tags, with sticky backs or with straight pins.
Handouts:	None
Pre-work:	None
Notes:	Feel free to make up your own names. Optionally, give a prize to the person who guesses their own character first.
Author/Source:	Unknown, adapted for Forum

Facilitator Preparation

Prepare name tags with the names of famous people or creatures. Here are some ideas:

Snow White	Abraham Lincoln	Mick Jagger	Dracula
Wizard of Oz	Ghandi	George W. Bush	Indiana Jones
Mickey Mouse	Shakespeare	Steven Spielberg	Frankenstein
Snoopy	Mother Teresa	Oprah Winfrey	Superman
Road Runner	Adolph Hitler	Donald Trump	Wonder Woman

Who Am I?, continued

Facilitator Instructions

1) Explain the objectives of the exercise and walk through the process.
2) Stick or pin a name tag on each person's back. Be sure the person doesn't see the name tag they've been given.
3) Instruct the participants that the goal is to figure out "who they are" by asking Yes/No questions to the other participants.
4) Guidelines:
   - You can ask only three questions per person before you must rotate to another person.
   - You can talk to the same person more than once.
   - Only ask Yes/No questions
5) Ask people to sit down when they have figured out who they are. They can continue to participate and help other people discover who they are.
6) Award a prize to the first and last person who guesses who they are.
7) As a group, discuss the questions provided below.

Discussion Questions:

a) What kinds of questions were most useful in identifying who your persona was?
b) Were non-verbal cues helpful in solving your task? Explain.
c) What did you learn about each other during this exercise?

Commonalities

The Commonalities exercises helps people learn more about each other in a fun, competitive manner. People are tasked with finding similarities with their fellow Forum members in a short period of time.

Objectives

- To loosen up, have fun
- To learn things about each other
- To underscore that people often have more in common than they think

Facilitator Info

Depth Level:	Light
Facilitation Skills:	Basic
Estimated Time:	20 minutes
Tools Needed:	Chairs—one for each person, bell timer
Handouts:	Commonalities Exercise Form
Pre-work:	None
Notes:	• Strive to find commonalities that you don't already know about each other • Try to find at least two commonalities per person • Optionally, give a prize to the person who gets the most commonalities
Author/Source:	Unknown, adapted for Forum

Facilitator Instructions

1) Arrange the chairs in pairs. If you have an odd number of people in the Forum, one person will have to sit out on each round.
2) Explain that the object of the exercise is to find as many common links between you and your fellow Forum members as possible.
3) Distribute copies of the Commonalities Exercise Form to each person.
4) Ask everyone to find a partner quickly. Set the timer for two minutes and tell them to start talking with their partner to identify commonalities. Write down the commonalities along with the person's name as you discover them.
5) When the timer signals the end of two minutes, everyone should quickly change seats to be with a different partner, and then set the timer again.
6) Repeat this process until everyone has met with everyone else in the Forum.
7) Finish with a discussion on the following questions:
   a. How many people found more than 20 commonalities?
   b. What were some of the most surprising items you discovered?
   c. What were some of the most unusual items you discovered?
   d. What implications does this exercise have for other group situations?

Commonalities, continued

Sample Commonalities

- We both have three children
- We are both Catholic
- Our fathers served in the military
- Our favorite subject in school was Chemistry
- Our favorite food is pizza
- Our favorite color is blue
- When we were little, we both wanted to be a doctor when we grew up
- We both played the violin as a kid
- We both voted Republican in the last presidential election
- We were both sprinters on the track team
- We've both been to a Rolling Stones concert
- Neither one of us graduated from college
- We both work out in the morning

Commonalities Exercise Form

	Commonality	Person's Name
1		
2		
3		
4		
5		
6		
7		
8		
9		
10		
11		
12		
13		
14		
15		
16		
17		
18		
19		
20		

Outer Limits

The Outer Limits exercise begins with a self-analysis on how comfortable we are in odd and unusual circumstances. The Forum compiles a series of ratings and discusses the implications behind what makes us uncomfortable or nervous.

Objectives

- To consider what makes us uncomfortable in front of other people and explore why we have those feelings
- To learn more about our fellow Forum members.

Facilitator Info

Depth Level:	Light
Facilitation Skills:	Basic
Estimated Time:	30 minutes
Tools Needed:	Flipchart, markers, pens/pencils
Handouts:	Outer Limits Worksheet (next page)
Pre-work:	None
Notes:	None
Author/Source:	"All Together Now", adapted for Forum

Facilitator Instructions

1) Distribute a copy of the Outer Limits Worksheet and a pencil to each Forum member.
2) Referring to the worksheet, explain that each person is to assume that they have been asked to do each of the ten listed activities alone, with the entire Forum as an audience. Ask them to number each activity according to the degree of discomfort it would cause them, with "1" being the most uncomfortable and "10" being the most comfortable.
3) After everyone has completed the worksheet, write the ten items on a flipchart and compile an average ranking for the listed items (add up the total of all members and divide by the number of members in the Forum). Write the average on the flipchart.
4) Ask each person to compare their individual rankings with the forum averages. Where there are large discrepancies, ask the individual to talk about why the discrepancy is so large. What makes them feel so uncomfortable, or why does something bother them less than it bothers other people?
5) Ask each person to actually perform one of the activities of their choice.
6) Discuss the following questions as a group:
   a. How did the overall Forum rankings compare to the individual rankings?
   b. What are some of the beliefs that would cause a person to feel uncomfortable or embarrassed in front of others?
   c. What are the sources of these beliefs?
   d. What is the relationship between actually *doing* these activities and *thinking* about having to do them?
   e. Would you feel equally uncomfortable if you were in front of a group of complete strangers? Your family? Your friends? Why?

Outer Limits Worksheet

Directions: Assume you were asked to do each of the following activities alone in front of the Forum. Number each activity according to the degree of discomfort it would cause you, with "1" being the most uncomfortable and "10" being the most comfortable.

_____   A. Oink like a pig.

_____   B. Dance.

_____   C. Tell a five-minute story about your personal life.

_____   D. Sing a song.

_____   E. Hug the person next to you.

_____   F. Stand with your back to someone of the opposite sex and hold hands.

_____   G. Strut around the room like a rooster.

_____   H. Act out a scene from Shakespeare.

_____   I. Read a love letter you have written to someone.

This or That?

This or That? is a fun exercise that helps Forum members learn about each other and what they have in common with each other. The exercise is highly interactive with people moving around the room to "speak with their feet".

Objectives

- To help Forum members see how they are different or similar to each other
- To loosen up and have fun

Facilitator Info

Depth Level:	Light
Facilitation Skills:	Basic
Estimated Time:	10 minutes
Tools Needed:	Wide open room setup, with no tables or chairs in the way. On one wall, place a sign that says THIS, and on the opposite wall place a sign that says THAT.
Handouts:	None
Pre-work:	None
Notes:	Feel free to add more THIS or THAT choices of your own.
Author/Source:	"Team Games for Trainers", adapted for Forum

Facilitator Instructions

1) Explain the purpose of the exercise. Tell members that they will "vote with their feet" by moving to one side of the room or the other, depending on the choice presented.
2) Ask the entire Forum to stand together as a group in the center of the room (this includes you as you are leading the exercise).
3) Now ask Forum members what they identify with more – This or That. A list is provided for you to read.
4) Keep the activity moving quickly. It will be a little chaotic and you may need to have a bell or whistle to get everyone's attention and move on.
5) Engage in a short debrief conversation using the questions below.

Debrief Questions

a) How did you feel about this exercise?
b) What surprised you?
c) Who surprised you?

This or That – Choices

	This	That
1	a BMW	a Toyota 4-Runner
2	Boston	San Francisco
3	a violet	a sunflower
4	popcorn	brownies
5	a waterfall	a river
6	a flute	a trombone
7	a dog	a cat
8	football	baseball
9	the beach	the park
10	classical music	rock and roll

	This	That
11	mountains	beach
12	sugar	salt
13	go	stop
14	the moon	the sun
15	summer	winter
16	right	left
17	a skateboard	a pogo stick
18	a power boat	a sailboat
19	wine	beer
20	a Big Mac	Dannon Yogurt

Unscrupulous!

How unscrupulous are you when it comes to making a moral decision? Everyone has their own inner voice; a line they won't cross. But, it's different for all. Unscrupulous! is an exercise that helps you find out just what that line is for other Forum members.

Objectives

- To learn more about your Forum members' ethics and opinions
- To learn how well you know your Forum members

Facilitator Info

Depth Level:	Medium
Facilitation Skills:	Basic
Estimated Time:	30 minutes
Tools Needed:	One set of 3x5 cards and one envelope for each person. A set consists of three cards with a single word written on each card – YES, NO, MAYBE. Use a bold marker pen so that the words are easy to read. Place the three cards in an envelope for each person.
Handouts:	None
Pre-work:	None
Notes:	<ul><li>When someone answers with "It depends," give them time to explain their answer.</li><li>You can create your own questions to add to this exercise.</li><li>Optionally, keep points for the most correct guesses and give a prize to the person with the most points at the end.</li></ul>
Author/Source:	Ellie Byrd

Facilitator Instructions

1) Explain the objectives of the exercise and walk through the process.
2) Distribute an envelope with three decision cards to each participant – Yes, No, Maybe.
3) Set the ground rules:
   a) Everyone must agree to be honest with their answers.
   b) You will read a question (see Questions below) for one of the participants. This person is in the "hot seat."
   c) The hot seat participant then chooses a decision card for his/her answer and places it face down in front of him/her. (Nobody else sees what they chose.)
   d) The other members select a decision card that represents how they THINK the participant has answered and places it face down in front of them.
   e) Everyone but the person in the hot seat reveals their cards.
   f) Then, the person in the hot seat reveals his/her card.
   g) If you are keeping score, people who have correctly guessed get a point. The person in the hot seat does not get a point when it is their own turn.
5) Repeat the process for all the participants and repeat for one or two more rounds.

Unscrupulous Questions

1. You discover that one of your key managers whom you regard as highly competent used false credentials during the interview process to get the job. Nobody else is aware of the infraction. Do you ignore the issue and keep the manager on the payroll?

2. Your brother-in-law is unfaithful to your sister. Do you tell your sister about it?

3. A neighbor gives you a key to their house to feed the cat while they're on vacation. When inside, do you wander around the house beyond what is necessary?

4. You have a wealthy aunt who is a pain in the neck. She is old and looking for heirs to whom she can leave her fortune. Do you treat her more kindly?

5. A friend who desperately needs a job applies at your company. Someone who is better qualified applies too. Do you hire your friend?

6. You are filling out your income tax form. Do you declare every cent you are supposed to declare?

7. You are sitting at a red light at 4 a.m. and there isn't a car in sight and there are no cameras. Do you go through the red light?

8. You're invited to a house party that turns into a skinny-dipping party in the host's back yard pool. Friends and strangers are present. Do you skinny-dip too?

9. You're backing out of a tight parking space at the shopping mall and you accidentally dent someone's car. Nobody has seen you. Do you leave a note taking responsibility?

10. Your 16-year-old daughter is a struggling actress. She has just been offered her first starring role in a major feature film, but she will have to do a love scene in the nude. Do you let her do it?

11. While on vacation in the Bahamas, you are walking along a deserted section of beach and you see a couple engaged in sex. Do you stay and watch?

12. Your business venture fails and you owe your creditors $1M. You can avoid payment by declaring bankruptcy. Do you?

13. You learn that your top salesperson lied on their resume about never being arrested. In fact, they have been arrested and served time for multiple DUIs. Nobody else is aware of the infraction and you haven't seen the person drinking excessively to-date. Do you ignore the issue and keep the salesperson on board?

14. You discover that your brother is selling classified information to a foreign country. Do you turn him in?

15. A friend who is a strict vegetarian is coming to dinner. You're feeling proud of the meal you have carefully planned around his vegetarian beliefs. Part way through dinner, you suddenly remember the beef stock you used to make the bean stew. Your guest is already eating it. Do you keep quiet and let him keep eating the bean stew?

16. A best friend's spouse is flirting with you at a party. Both of your spouses are there, but they are out of the room and haven't seen it. Do you tell your spouse about it?

17. You know you are attractive and so does your prospective customer. Do you lightly flirt to get a major new account for your business?

18. You discover that your spouse once appeared in a porno film – long before you met. Do you stay with him/her?

19. You're playing a card game and you accidentally see an opponent's hand. Do you say so?

20. You're out to dinner with clients and you see a friend's spouse in a romantic tryst with an unknown person. Do you mention what you saw to your friend?

Unscrupulous Questions, continued

21. The taxi driver gives you a blank receipt as he drops you off. You are on an expense account. Do you report the exact, correct amount?

22. A vagrant asks you for $20. You suspect he/she will spend it on drugs or alcohol. Do you give it anyway?

23. The elections are coming up and you dislike all of the political candidates. Do you vote?

24. Your friend, a lawyer, is having personal problems that are affecting his work. Do you take your business elsewhere until he works out his problems?

25. You're at an important business dinner and your client has a large piece of spinach stuck between his teeth. Every time he smiles or laughs, you can't help but see it. Do you tell him about the spinach?

26. You're bidding on a large project against several competitors. Your customer wants you to win the bid and offers to show you the bids of your competitors. Do you accept the offer to see the other bids?

27. A good friend has been unemployed for several months. They ask you to write a reference for a job that you don't think they're well qualified for. Do you write the reference?

28. You are invited to invest in a company that does well because of its monopoly, however, they make a poor product. Do you invest?

29. You've purchased an expensive set of luggage at a major department store and charged it on your credit card. After several months, you realize that the charge has never been billed to your account. Do you report the mistake?

30. You discover that your spouse is a practicing bisexual. Do you stay with him/her?

31. The economy is bad and you're struggling financially. You are offered $500,000 to endorse a product that you dislike and would NEVER use. Do you endorse it?

32. You've boarded the plane and settled into a comfortable bulkhead seat with lots of leg room for a 5-hour flight. An elderly man approaches and asks you if you'll change seats with his wife so that they can sit together. You would have to move to a center seat on another row. Do you move?

33. Your 12 year-old son asks you to buy Penthouse magazine for him. Do you?

34. You're golfing with an important client who thinks that golf skills are as important as business skills. Your ball has a bad lie, but you can move it to a better position without being seen. Do you?

35. Your 16 year-old son drives home and is obviously drunk. In fact, he is so drunk he doesn't remember how he crashed the front end of the car. Based on the damage, it appears that he was in an accident with another car. Do you turn him in to the police?

36. A fellow Forum member has bad breath. Do you tell him/her?

37. You're eating at a restaurant and the service is terrible. After endless delays, the waitress brings you the wrong meal and the food is cold. Do you demand a new dinner?

38. You're on vacation, and your spouse is off snorkeling while you relax in the hot tub. An extremely attractive man/woman joins you in the hot tub and starts a friendly conversation. A few minutes later the attractive person accidentally brushes against your leg and a few minutes after that they offer to buy you a drink. Do you accept?

39. Your aging, negative, handicapped mother wants to move in with you and your spouse. Do you let her?

40. A friend confides to you that he has committed a crime and makes you promise to never tell. Now you've found out that an innocent person has been accused of the crime, and you beg your friend to give himself up. He refuses, reminding you of your original promise. Do you turn him in anyway?

Unscrupulous Questions, Continued

41. You win a substantial amount of money on the lottery but a relative who you dislike is in serious debt. Do you keep the win a secret from your whole family?

42. You are the last hope for a distant relative who urgently needs a bone-marrow donation but there is a 20% chance you won't survive the operation. Would you agree to the donation?

43. Your best friend asks you to stand as guarantor of a $75,000 loan. If they don't get the loan their house will be repossessed. Would you be willing to take the risk considering that if they default, you become liable for the debt?

44. You enter a quiz and the winning team will be awarded $20,000 for the charity of their choice. You find a copy of the questions before the quiz. Is it okay to cheat for the benefit of a charity?

45. You've been speeding and a policeman pulls you over. Do you make up a lie to try to get out of the ticket?

46. One of your friends occasionally has body odor. You ignored a couple of times hoping it was an isolated incident but it's been happening more often. Do you tell him?

47. A friend has been working on writing a book for three years. Finally, he gives you a draft copy of the book and asks you to read it and give him feedback. You read the first chapter and it's TERRIBLE! Do you tell your friend the truth about how bad the book is?

48. You helped your son write his book report, in fact, you basically wrote it for him. His teacher is suspicious and asks your son if you helped him and he denies it. Now, the teacher calls you to ask you directly if you wrote it. Do you admit that you did?

49. You see some great content that you can use for a presentation, but you know it's copyrighted. Do you use the content without getting permission?

50. Your dog gets really sick. The vet tells you that your dog will surely die, but there's one possible hope... a $10,000 operation that has a 60% success rate in similar cases. Do you proceed with the operation?

Communication Starters

Communication Starters are questions or phrases that help people share information about themselves. In this exercise, questions are divided into three levels, with each level increasing in depth and intensity. Questions are often used at the start of a retreat, a retreat segment or meeting. They can also be used throughout the retreat at random times.

Objectives

- To learn more about each other
- To discuss topics that may not come up in everyday conversation
- To bring focus to the present moment
- To feel more connected and "on the same page" with fellow Forum members
- To transition into the Forum frame of mind (more introspective)

Facilitator Info

Depth Level:	Varies
Facilitation Skills:	Basic
Estimated Time:	15 minutes
Tools Needed:	List of Communication Starters (next page)
Handouts:	None
Pre-work:	None
Notes:	• The terms "Communication Starter" and "Ice Breaker" are often used interchangeably. • Many Forums start every meeting with a Communication Starter. • Some Forums use Communications Starters throughout their retreat. • To add a level of surprise to the exercise, write questions on slips of paper and let people draw their question out of a hat. • Select the appropriate level of Communication Starter based on your Forum's level of depth. • If you are seeking a higher level of depth, consider going first yourself and lead by example. In other words, share something highly private or personal to set the example for others to follow.
Author/Source:	Ellie Byrd

Facilitator Instructions

1) Decide which level of question is appropriate for your Forum.
2) Choose between Option A and Option B.
   a. Option A – Select a single question and ask everyone to answer the same question.
   b. Option B – Select a different question for each person to answer.
3) Thank each person for sharing their answer, especially after the deeper, Level 3 questions.

Communication Starters – Level 1

Level 1 Ice Breakers are appropriate for new Forums, or Forums that have just brought in new members. They may also be used by older Forums to bring some levity to the meeting. The questions tend to be light-hearted, but don't be surprised if a Level 1 question leads to a much deeper answer than you expect!

1) As a child, my favorite game was _____
2) My favorite movie of all time is _____
3) Today, I have the most fun when _____
4) I would be the happiest person in the world if I had _____
5) I will eat anything put in front of me except _____
6) I can explain my life as an animal and that animal is a _____
7) If I had all the money in the world, I would _____
8) School for me was _____
9) If I had to give up some modern convenience, like TV, car, cell phone, indoor plumbing or electricity, I would give up _____
10) If I had to choose between losing my hearing or sight, I would choose _____
11) If you could be a character in a book or novel, who would you be and why?
12) If you had the option to live in any period in history, what era would you select and why?
13) If you could re-live your childhood in some other country than your own, what country would you choose and why?
14) List three things that bring you energy. List three things that drain your energy.
15) How attentive are you to your physical health?
16) If you could speak one language other than your native language, what would it be and why?
17) You are in the library that is burning down and you can only save two books. Which two do you choose? What would the world lose if those two books were gone?
18) What is the most transformative travel experience you have ever had? What made it so transformational?
19) A gift I can give to others is _____
20) A gift I would like to receive from others is _____
21) What makes me laugh is _____
22) Talk about a mistake you recently made.
23) If you could magically have 2 more hours every day (26 hour day), what would you do with the extra time?
24) If you suddenly lost 2 hours every day (a 22 hour day), what would you cut out of your current schedule to accommodate for the lost time?
25) Assume you have absolutely NO restrictions and you could live anywhere in the world. Where would you live and why? What restrictions did you have to "remove" from your thought process in order to live there?
26) What was the last book that you read, cover to cover? Why did you read it? What did you learn from it? Would you recommend it to others?
27) Share something mischievous you did as a child.
28) Your home is about to be hit by a tornado! You have 10 minutes to grab a few things and get out. What would you take?
29) What is the most surprising thing you have learned about your childhood?
30) Name something that happened in the last 90 days that you are proud of.

Communication Starters – Level 1, continued

31) Which holiday has the most meaning to you? Why?

32) Complete the sentence: "I wish all people would _____"

33) Describe the perfect vacation for you.

34) Name three things about yourself that you like the best.

35) What dream do you have that you wish would become a reality?

36) If you had one wish that was guaranteed to come true, what would you wish for and why?

37) How many hours of TV do you watch each week? In what way does TV influence your life?

38) What would you like to be doing five years from now? What do you think you'll be doing five years from now?

39) Do you feel mastery in any part of your life? If so, where?

40) My most prized possession (material item) is _____

41) If someone were to write a biography about you, what would the title be?

42) If you could change one physical feature about yourself, what would you change and why?

43) Imagine that you are going to be stranded on a desert island with two people for the rest of your life. Who are the two people you would choose to take with you and why?

Communication Starters – Level 2

Level 2 Ice Breakers are appropriate for Forums that have been together for a while – one or more years. In order for people to be completely open and honest with their answers, they must have a strong level of trust in confidentiality and the Forum must have achieved good depth in conversations.

1) If I could throw caution to the wind and really take a risk, I would _____
2) I cry when _____
3) If you could choose a second set of parents in addition to your own, who would you choose and why? What does each of these people bring or contribute to you?
4) How many of your friendships have lasted more than 10 years? Which of your current friends do you think will be important to you 10 years from now?
5) Describe what would be a perfect day for you, from beginning to end.
6) If you were magically granted the one talent of your dreams, what would it be? How would that change your life?
7) How do you react to difficult situations in your life?
8) Describe your relationship with your mother today. What was it like growing up?
9) Describe your relationship with your father today. What was it like growing up?
10) Do you feel you are a good parent? What do you do well and what could you do better as a parent?
11) Can you be counted on to do what you say you will do? What does it take for you to trust someone?
12) Name one thing you could do to improve an important relationship in your life.
13) What could you stop doing now that would benefit your own growth and well-being?
14) Imagine that you could go back in time and change one decision in your life. What decision would you change and why?
15) Who is someone that you would like to apologize to but haven't? What is the situation? Why haven't you apologized?
16) Who is someone that owes an apology to you? What is the situation? Why do you think they haven't apologized to you yet?
17) What is your exit strategy for your business?
18) Summarize your childhood in 3 words.
19) Is it easy for you to accept help when you need it? Do you ask for help when you need it?
20) Think back to when you were a child. What did you think your life would be like when you grew up? What were your dreams? Have any of them come true?
21) Think of a positive or negative remark that was said to you as a child. How did it affect you then? What is the impact of it on you now?
22) When was the last time you felt intimidated or insecure? Why do you think you felt that way?
23) What has been the greatest joy in your life?
24) What are you doing to help your children build their own values and beliefs?
25) What are your most compulsive habits? How do you handle these?
26) When is the last time you were in a fight with someone? Who caused it? Who won?
27) Talk about a time when you have lost your temper.
28) What has been your greatest success? Your greatest failure?
29) What is the single best decision you have made in your business?
30) What is the single best decision you have made in your life?

Communication Starters – Level 2, continued

31) When was the first time you fell in love? Why did you fall in love with this person and how long did you stay in love?

32) Generally, do you think you are a good judge of character? Think of a time when you were wrong about someone's character and describe the situation.

33) Imagine you are diagnosed with a rare disease. You have a choice between living healthy for one more year, or unhealthy (dependent on medication and the help of others) for 10 more years. Which would you choose and why?

34) Think of the photograph that means the most to you. Describe the photo and explain why it means so much to you.

35) If, by magic, you could change one thing about yourself or your life, what would you change?

36) Share a childhood experience with death.

37) What keeps you up at night – business, personal or family related?

38) Describe your parents in two sentences – one sentence for your mom, one sentence for your dad.

39) What is one thing you could do to improve your business?

40) What is the most risky decision you ever made in your life? What made the risk so great?

41) On a scale of 1 to 10, rate how balanced you think your life is. Name one thing you could do to improve the balance.

Communication Starters – Level 3

Level 3 Ice Breakers are appropriate for strong, healthy Forums that have been together for a while (several years). These types of questions lead to introspective thinking and they can generate deep emotions.

1) The most important decision in my life was/is _____
2) What I need to make my life complete is _____ because _____
3) What are your top 5 priorities in life?
4) If I suddenly found out that I had 24 hours to live, I would spend them doing _____
5) Share something that you have never told anyone before.
6) What has been the greatest disappointment in your life?
7) Describe your spiritual life in 3 words.
8) Have you ever hated anyone? Why and for how long?
9) Name someone who helped you (not a relative) when you were a child. What did they do to help you?
10) Share an experience when you felt ashamed.
11) What is your greatest fear in life?
12) Describe the best day of your life. Describe the worst day of your life.
13) When was the last time you cried when you were by yourself? What was the situation?
14) If you were to die tomorrow, what three things would you NOT have accomplished that you wish you had?
15) When was the last time someone hurt you emotionally? Describe the situation.
16) Describe the funeral service you would like to have held for you.
17) Imagine that you could have a panel of three people to help you with your most important decisions. Who are the three people you would want on your panel and why would you choose them? (These people may be living or dead.)
18) When do you feel most lonely?
19) Of all people close to you, whose death would you find most disturbing? Why?
20) What do you like best about your life? Least about your life?
21) What are your beliefs about a "higher power"?
22) If you were to die this evening with no opportunity to communicate with anyone, what would you most regret not having told someone?
23) What has been the most difficult period in your life?
24) What is your most treasured memory?
25) What would you like your legacy to be?
26) Who is the most significant person in your life? Why?
27) What is your biggest regret?
28) If you could ask God one question, what would you ask?
29) Who is the one person who has done the most to make you who you are today? How was that person significant to you?
30) So far in your life, whose death has been the most difficult for you to accept? What has been so difficult about it?
31) If you could identify one main thing that is holding you back from being all that you can and want to be, what is that one main thing? What is holding you back?

Category 3
Forum Assessments

Use an assessment to gauge the health of your Forum. Many Forums conduct an assessment each year to measure progress and identify opportunities for improvement

Refer to Part 1 of this book, Planning Your Retreat, for information on how to facilitate exercises. Time estimates for individual exercises are based on an 8-person Forum. Adjust the time estimates as needed to accommodate the size of your Forum.

Category 3 Exercises

forumsherpa

Annual Alignment (The Three B's)

Annual Alignment is an exercise that Forums run annually to assess what will bring value to the Forum members over the coming year. The exercise prompts a discussion on how to fulfill the value proposition for all members, despite differing needs. The results of this exercise can be used to establish a focus for the coming year, identify topical discussions, select guest speakers and periodically engage in exercises.

Objectives

- To assess what brings value to each person in the Forum
- To discuss alignment of Forum members on Forum take-away value
- To consider the skills, talents, knowledge and resources that each member can bring to the Forum
- To consider the skills, talents, knowledge and resources that each member would like to get from the Forum

Facilitator Info

Depth Level:	Intermediate
Facilitation Skills:	Medium
Estimated Time:	10 minutes to complete the worksheet and 30 minutes to share responses and discuss alignment
Tools Needed:	Flipchart, paper, pens/pencils
Handouts:	Three B's Worksheet
Pre-work:	None
Notes:	Be sure everyone writes down their responses in silence before you begin to share ratings and responses.
Author/Source:	Unknown, adapted for Forum

Facilitator Instructions

1) Explain the concept of the Three B's.
2) Distribute The Three B's Worksheet and ask people to think about what will bring them value over the coming year. Allow 5 to 10 minutes for people to complete the worksheet – both the numeric ratings and the Forum Take-Away Value questions.
3) Draw three columns on a flipchart for the 3 B's. Ask each person to share their numbers and their thoughts behind the numbers. Write the numbers on the flipchart.
4) After everyone has shared their numbers, look at the results. Are people generally aligned? Where are the potential misalignments? As a Forum, how can the group satisfy the needs of everyone?
5) Ask each person to share their answers to the Forum Take-Away Value Questions.
6) Facilitate discussion on how the Forum can meet the needs of the members while capitalizing on what the members can offer.

Annual Alignment – Sample of the Three B's

Name	Business	Balance	Buddies
Joe	50%	25%	25%
Peter	60%	10%	30%
Morgan	80%	10%	10%
Maria	40%	50%	10%
Steve	40%	20%	40%
Simon	70%	15%	15%
Paul	20%	20%	60%
Claude	60%	20%	20%

In this example, most of the Forum members are focused on Business Growth. Paul is more interested in Buddies, and he is the only person who doesn't have Business listed as his primary focus. This could prompt a discussion on how the Forum will meet his interest in social/friendship needs. Meanwhile, Morgan and Simon are highly focused on Business Growth. Are they comfortable with non-business conversations and presentations?

Annual Check
Note that this exercise can be repeated annually as an alignment check. People's ratings will change from year to year, depending on what is happening in their life. Life changes may cause us to shift what we want to get out of the Forum and how the Forum can bring us value.

Physical Variation
Imagine a large, invisible triangle on the floor. Place a sign at each angle on the triangle – one for Business, one for Balance, one for Buddies. (You can place a chair at each angle of the triangle and tape a piece of paper on each chair back with the word – Business, Balance, or Buddies.) Then ask people to physically position themselves within the boundaries of the triangle to represent where they want to get value from the Forum over the next year. E.g., if you want equal parts from each of the 3 B's, you'd position yourself exactly in the middle of the triangle. If you want more business take-away value, move yourself toward the chair that represents Business. After everyone has positioned themselves, ask them to look around at where others are standing. Then, each person talks about why they're standing where they are.

Annual Alignment (The Three B's) Worksheet

Forum value typically comes from a combination of three areas (the three B's):

a) **Business** – I want to grow my business and I'm looking for wisdom, experiences and input to help me do that. I see the Forum as a source of knowledge, resources, accountability and/or shared information that will help me with this.

b) **Balance** – I'm looking for balance in my life. This is a holistic view of my life as a person and a business leader. It encompasses my sense of inner peace, commitment to family, living healthy, fulfilling my purpose, etc. I would like the Forum to support me as I seek to achieve balance in these areas.

c) **Buddies** – I'm looking for friendships. I enjoy socializing with my peers. I'm so busy with work, I neglect my friends at times. I would like to build long-lasting interpersonal relationships with the members of my Forum.

Write down how important each of the three B's are to you in the space below. Think about what you want gain from the Forum over the coming year. What will bring you value? Use a numeric percentage, assigning a value to each of the three B's with a total of 100%.

Business _____   Balance _____   Buddies _____

Forum Take-Away Value Questions

What specific skills, talents, resources or knowledge do you believe you can offer to the Forum?

What specific skills, talents, resources or knowledge would you like to get from the Forum?

Forum Member Assessment

The Forum Member Assessment is a tool to raise awareness of how individual members can contribute to the overall success of the Forum. Based on Aristotle's theory that "the whole is greater than the sum of its parts", each member should be aware of how important their individual contribution is.

Objectives

- To raise awareness among all Forum members about how they can be a strong, contributing participant in the Forum
- To help Forum members look at their own behaviors and determine if they are contributing or detracting from the Forum experience for the entire group

Facilitator Info

Depth Level:	Light
Facilitation Skills:	Medium
Estimated Time:	20 minutes
Tools Needed:	Flipchart, markers, paper, pens/pencils
Handouts:	None
Pre-work:	None
Notes:	It is best to do this exercise with people who have been in the Forum for at least two years.
Author/Source:	Ellie Byrd

Facilitator Instructions

1) Discuss how important our words, actions and behaviors are in the Forum and how they can impact the health of the Forum. Each individual person has the opportunity to contribute to the health of the Forum, and at the same time each individual person can detract from the health of the Forum.
2) Give everyone a blank sheet of paper and a pen. Ask them to draw a line down the middle of the page.
3) On the left side of the page, ask them to write down three traits or characteristics that they feel make a strong Forum member. You may want to suggest that they think of the strongest Forum member they've seen; then think of three things that person does that makes them such a strong member.
4) On the right side of the page, ask them to write down three traits or characteristics that make a weak Forum member. Again, it may help for them to picture the weakest Forum member they've ever seen and write down three things that make them such a weak Forum member.
5) Give people several minutes to think in silence about the traits and write them down.
6) On a flipchart page, draw a line down the center. One at a time, ask each person to share the characteristics they wrote down. Write their answers on the flipchart in the appropriate column. Add a tick mark next to the ones that are mentioned more than once.
7) At the end of the exercise, ask everyone to look at the list of strong characteristics. Ask them to think about their own actions in the Forum and whether they demonstrate those characteristics. Likewise, ask them to think about the list of weak characteristics and consider whether they demonstrate any of those behaviors.
8) Allow for discussion to pop up naturally, but don't engage in finger-pointing or accusations. The intent of the exercise is self-discovery and self-awareness.

Teamwork Survey

The Teamwork Survey provides a 15-point health check for the Forum, focused on effective team skills.

Objectives

- To assess member views of the Forum's ability to function as a team
- To raise awareness of Forum strengths and opportunities for improvement

Facilitator Info

Depth Level:	Light
Facilitation Skills:	Medium
Estimated Time:	30 minutes to 1 hour
Tools Needed:	Flipchart, markers, pens/pencils
Handouts:	Copies of Teamwork Survey Form
Pre-work:	None
Notes:	To save time, the survey can be run in advance using an electronic survey tool.
Author/Source:	Ellie Byrd

Facilitator Instructions

1) Distribute copies of the Teamwork Survey and ask Forum members to complete it. The survey should be anonymous so don't write names on them.
2) Collect the forms and compile the data.
3) Discuss the survey results. Write key points and decisions on the flipchart.
   a. Where are we particularly strong as a Forum?
   b. Where are there are opportunities for improvement?
   c. What kinds of changes could we consider to improve our teamwork as a Forum?

Teamwork Survey Form
Circle one choice for each question.

1) Does the Forum have a clear vision and mission?
   a) We have no clear vision or mission.
   b) I'm not sure about the vision and mission.
   c) I'm fairly sure about the vision and mission.
   d) We have a clear vision and mission that we defined as a group.
2) Does the Forum have an effective constitution that defines group norms, processes and protocols?
   a) We don't have a Forum constitution.
   b) Our Forum constitution is weak.
   c) Our Forum constitution is pretty good.
   d) We have a strong Forum constitution.
3) Are there clear goals for the Forum?
   a) We have no stated goals.
   b) I'm not sure about the goals of the Forum.
   c) I'm fairly sure about the goals of the Forum.
   d) We have clear goals that we defined as a group and we monitor regularly.
4) Describe the typical participation pattern in Forum meetings.
   a) A few people consistently dominate.
   b) Participation varies from topic to topic.
   c) Everyone plays an equal role.
5) How much honesty and openness is there in the Forum?
   a) People hide what they really think.
   b) We are somewhat open.
   c) We are quite open.
   d) We are totally open and honest.
6) How good are members at listening, supporting, respecting and encouraging each other?
   a) We don't do this at all.
   b) We try but we don't always succeed.
   c) We are fairly skilled at this.
   d) We are consistently excellent
7) How do members handle differences of opinion?
   a) We get emotional and often argue.
   b) It varies
   c) We always debate objectively and respectfully
8) How are important decisions usually made?
   a) One person decides.
   b) We vote.
   c) We seek compromise.
   d) We work together to reach consensus.
9) How would you describe the Forum meetings?
   a) Unstructured, waste of time
   b) Average value
   c) Good value, but not consistently so
   d) Well planned and productive

Teamwork Survey Form, continued

10) Does the Forum usually end its meetings with a sense of achievement?
   a) Never
   b) Rarely
   c) Sometimes
   d) Usually
   e) Always

11) How would you describe the relationship between members during the Forum meetings?
   a) Strained and tense
   b) Satisfactory
   c) Good
   d) Totally harmonious

12) How would you describe the relationship between members outside the Forum meetings?
   a) We never communicate outside the Forum meetings.
   b) We see and talk only on rare occasions.
   c) We see and talk periodically.
   d) We see and talk to each other frequently outside the Forum meetings.

13) When action is planned, are clear role assignments made and accepted?
   a) Never
   b) Sometimes
   c) Always

14) Does the Forum ever stop and evaluate how it's doing, and then take action to improve?
   a) Never
   b) Rarely
   c) Periodically
   d) Consistently

15) How committed are the members to the Forum?
   a) Low level of commitment
   b) Inconsistent level of commitment
   c) Average level of commitment
   d) Strong level of commitment

Mission, Vision, Values and Goals

Mission, Vision, Values and Goals is an exercise that helps the Forum identify, discuss and document its heart and soul. Through a series of guided discussions, Forum member will identify their Vision Statement, Mission Statement, Core Values and Forum Goals.

Objectives

- To discuss and achieve alignment among Forum members on the mission, vision, values and goals of the Forum
- To practice using a variety of techniques to achieve group alignment

Facilitator Info

Depth Level:	Medium
Facilitation Skills:	Medium
Estimated Time:	2 hours
Tools Needed:	Flipchart, markers
Handouts:	None
Pre-work:	None
Notes:	Consider adding the vision and mission statement to the beginning of your Forum constitution and to the top of every meeting agenda.
Author/Source:	Ellie Byrd

Facilitator Instructions

Part 1: Group Vision

The Group Vision should reflect the collective views of all Forum members as to why the Forum exists. This is generally one or two sentences. It defines who you are as a Forum and what brings value to the individual members of the Forum. It is a long-term, high-level view. For most Forums, the vision never changes.

Example: "Our vision is to learn, share and support each other in achieving our respective professional and personal goals. Our Forum is a unique, safe environment where we can be completely open and honest."

1) Appoint a scribe to collect ideas.
2) Using a flipchart or white board, collect ideas from all Forum members. The scribe writes down each idea for everyone to see.
   a. Be inclusive. All members should contribute at least one idea.
   b. There is no such thing as a bad idea. Write down every idea.
   c. Don't write down names. The idea is what's important, not who provided it.
   d. Don't engage in a discussion about an idea during this section, simply collect the ideas.
3) Discuss the ideas.
   a. Are there any ideas that are duplicates?
   b. Are there any ideas that need clarification? Does everyone understand the meaning of all the ideas? Does an idea need to be re-worded?
   c. Are there any ideas that need to be removed? Does anyone disagree with a particular idea?
   d. Are there any ideas that can be merged into one idea?

Mission, Vision, Values and Goals, continued

Part 1: Vision, continued

4) Re-write the list into a concise form. If there are more than 5 ideas on the list, it's time to identify the top 5 ideas.
   a. Ask each person to vote for their top 3 most important ideas. Do this by having the Forum members come to the board one at a time, give them a marker, and ask them to vote by placing a tick mark beside their favorite 3 ideas.
   b. After all votes are completed, determine the top 5 ideas. If you need to break a tie, have the Forum members vote one more time – just on the tie breaker.
5) Take the top five ideas and construct one or two sentences that incorporate all ideas.
   a. This should be a free-form, group effort.
   b. Be sure to include all five of the vision ideas.
   c. Be sure everyone agrees on the final vision statement. Note that the statement can be more than one sentence. But try not to be too verbose. Less is more. Write the Vision Statement here:

Part 2: Group Mission

The Group Mission Statement represents what the group aspires to be. The mission statement reflects where the Forum sees itself in a short term time frame (one or two years).

Example: "One year from now, our Forum will be having deep and substantial presentations and our trust in confidentiality will be total and unquestionable. Our Forum will be a significant, valuable part of each member's life."

1) Split the Forum into groups of three or four people.
2) Ask each group to develop a mission statement. Allow approximately 10 minutes for this.
3) Ask each group to select a spokesman and have the spokesman present their mission statement.
4) Engage in a discussion of the two mission statements, with a goal of merging them into a single statement.
   a. Eliminate any duplications between the two statements.
   b. Discuss and remove any segments that are not supported by everyone.
   c. Wordsmith the remaining statements until you reach your final group mission statement. Note that the statement can be more than one sentence. Write it here:

Mission, Vision, Values and Goals, continued

Part 3: Values

Forum Values should reflect the core beliefs of all members in the Forum.

Example: Honesty, Compassion, Life Balance

1) Distribute 5 blank 3 x 5 cards to each person.
2) Ask each person to write down five values that they would like their Forum to embrace, one on each card. They do not need to write their name on the card. Allow 5 to 10 minutes for this.
3) Collect all the cards and mix them up.
4) Use a flipchart and write down each value. When a value appears more than once, add a tick mark to indicate additional votes.
5) As a group, discuss which values are similar enough that they can be merged. Be sure to transfer the tick marks.
6) Discuss any values that the group questions or does not support. Remove these values if needed.
7) Determine the top five values based on the number of votes for each one. Write them here:

```
┌─────────────────────────────────────────────────────────────────────────┐
│                                                                           │
│                                                                           │
│                                                                           │
│                                                                           │
│                                                                           │
│                                                                           │
└─────────────────────────────────────────────────────────────────────────┘
```

Part 4: Goals

Forum Goals should be set annually to help Forum members increase the value of their Forum experience while working as a team to achieve the selected goals.

Examples: We will have 100% attendance at all meetings, we will increase our presentation depth from 6.2 to 8.0 or higher, each member will meet at least once with each other member outside the Forum meeting, we won't lose any members, we'll have 2 social events outside our meetings, etc.

1) Ask each person to think of three goals that they would like the Forum to aspire to achieve over the next year.
2) Go around the room and ask each person to share their three goals. Scribe the goals on a flipchart.
3) If a goal is repeated, do not write it down twice.
4) After all the goals are written down, have each person vote for their top 3 goals by raising their hand when the goal is read.
5) Determine the top 5 or 6 goals, then have a second vote, again asking each person to vote on their top 3 choices.
6) Transcribe the final three goals to a separate page and write them here:

```
┌─────────────────────────────────────────────────────────────────────────┐
│                                                                           │
│                                                                           │
│                                                                           │
│                                                                           │
│                                                                           │
└─────────────────────────────────────────────────────────────────────────┘
```

7) Consider adding the goals to the top of your meeting agenda every month. You may also want to add the Forum vision, mission and values to the agenda.

Moderator Scorecard

The Moderator Scorecard provides the moderator with valuable insights from the Forum on how they're doing in their role as Moderator. By reviewing the self-assessment and the input from the Forum, the moderator can consider possible changes to their style and/or actions as a moderator.

Objectives

- To provide input to the moderator on ten leadership skills
- To offer appreciation and support to the moderator

Facilitator Info

Depth Level:	Light
Facilitation Skills:	Basic
Estimated Time:	1 hour
Tools Needed:	Pens/pencils
Handouts:	Moderator Scorecard Worksheet
Pre-work:	None
Notes:	To save time, use an automated survey tool to gather scorecard information anonymously. Consider whether you will be comfortable reading the responses (regardless of how positive or negative they may be!) if you decide to use this exercise.
Author/Source:	Ellie Byrd

Facilitator Instructions

1) First, assess your perception of your own skills by completing the Scorecard for yourself.
2) Next, have a candid discussion with your Forum about the Scorecard and its purpose. Assure them that their responses will be held in complete confidence and that you will be using their input for your own self-improvement. The main purpose is for you to understand their perceptions and thereby improve the Forum experience for all members.
3) Distribute a copy of the Scorecard to all Forum members and ask them to complete the form. This is best done at the end of the Forum meeting during Housekeeping functions.
4) Collect the responses and wait until after the meeting to review them on your own.
5) You may want to make a list of areas of where you feel you want to make changes, as well as a list of the areas where your own perceptions are vastly different from the perception of your Forum members. Consider how you might want to make changes in your style. You may want to share your plans with the Forum and ask them for their help in specific areas if appropriate.

Moderator Scorecard Worksheet

Circle a number from one to ten to indicate your impressions of the current moderator's skills and handling of the Forum. If a topic is not applicable, skip the question.

	low, weak								high, strong	
Clarity and communication of Forum vision	1	2	3	4	5	6	7	8	9	10
Organization and planning skills	1	2	3	4	5	6	7	8	9	10
Listening skills	1	2	3	4	5	6	7	8	9	10
Communication clarity and consistency	1	2	3	4	5	6	7	8	9	10
Compassion when needed	1	2	3	4	5	6	7	8	9	10
Firmness when needed	1	2	3	4	5	6	7	8	9	10
Decision-making skills	1	2	3	4	5	6	7	8	9	10
Conflict resolution skills	1	2	3	4	5	6	7	8	9	10
Commitment to Forum	1	2	3	4	5	6	7	8	9	10
Modeling the desired behaviors	1	2	3	4	5	6	7	8	9	10

Optionally, name one thing that this moderator does particularly well:

_____

Optionally, name one area where this moderator could improve:

_____

Forum Vitality Survey

The Forum Vitality Survey provides a simple method of assessing Forum Health. Based on a collection 12 thought-provoking questions, the Forum can quickly identify potential challenges and opportunities for improvement.

Objectives

- To assess member views of the Forum
- To raise awareness of Forum strengths and opportunities for improvement

Facilitator Info

Depth Level:	Medium
Facilitation Skills:	Medium
Estimated Time:	<ul><li>10 minutes to complete the survey</li><li>20 minutes to compile the survey results</li><li>30 minutes to discuss strengths and weaknesses</li></ul>
Tools Needed:	Flipchart, markers
Handouts:	Forum Vitality Survey form (next 2 pages)
Pre-work:	None
Notes:	Many Forums perform this survey annually and save the results in order to have an ongoing record of the Forum's health and life cycle. Optionally, this survey can be administered in advance using an online survey tool.
Author/Source:	Joan Mara

Facilitator Instructions

1) Give each member a copy of the survey. Tell them the survey is meant to be anonymous so they should NOT write their name on it.
2) Ask each person to circle the number that most closely represents their impressions of the Forum.
3) After about 10 minutes, collect the forms and tabulate the results.
4) Share the results with the Forum members (write on flipchart).
5) Lead the Forum in a discussion of strengths and opportunities for improvement. Ideally, select three areas where the Forum would like to improve over the next year.

Forum Vitality Survey Form

1.   Attendance and Punctuality

      1   2   3   4   5   6   7   8   9   10

Members arrive late and leave early. Absenteeism is high with a different group of members each meeting.

100% attendance with members arriving on time and remaining for the entire meeting.

2.   Schedule/Format

      1   2   3   4   5   6   7   8   9   10

No clear beginning or end to meetings, with a great deal of time wasted.

Meetings start and end on schedule, with no time wasted.

3.   Retreats

      1   2   3   4   5   6   7   8   9   10

Never had a retreat; or retreats are superficial, poorly attended and a waste of time.

Held annual retreat with 100% attendance. Retreats are valuable and assist in the bonding of members.

4.   Confidentiality

      1   2   3   4   5   6   7   8   9   10

I will never disclose anything of a truly confidential nature to this group for fear of leaks.

I feel totally confident that nothing discussed in our meetings will ever be disclosed outside of the Forum.

5.   Conflicts of Interest

      1   2   3   4   5   6   7   8   9   10

There are conflicts of interest which limit the openness of discussions.

There are no conflicts of interest. Complete freedom for open discussion exists.

6.   Knowledge/Understanding of Forum Colleagues

      1   2   3   4   5   6   7   8   9   10

I have no idea of the background, values, or motivation of other members.

I have a great deal of knowledge and understanding of fellow Forum members.

7.   Trust

      1   2   3   4   5   6   7   8   9   10

I feel uncomfortable disclosing personal or confidential information.

I feel totally comfortable disclosing even the most personal, embarrassing, or confidential information in our Forum.

8.   Presentations

      1   2   3   4   5   6   7   8   9   10

Presentations are mostly "show and tell" descriptions of how the business works or "happiness reports" about the family.

Presentations deal with presenter feelings and involve significant unresolved questions requiring meaningful input.

Forum Vitality Survey Form, continued

9.   Presenters

1	2	3	4	5	6	7	8	9	10

Presenters are unprepared and have
unclear objectives and expectations.

Presenters are well prepared
and clearly state their objectives
and expectations.

10.   Group Discussion

1	2	3	4	5	6	7	8	9	10

One member is allowed to dominate
discussions, members are judgmental,
and focus on "fixing" the person and/or
"solving" the problems.

All members get involved
in discussions. Focusing first
on the presenter's feelings then
ask thought-provoking questions
to help the presenter find his/her
own answers.

11.   Group Moderator

1	2	3	4	5	6	7	8	9	10

Is ineffective. Fails to provide
focus or direction for the meeting.

Skillful at facilitating meeting.
Encourages members to participate,
creates safe environment, models
communication protocol.

12.   Meeting My Needs

1	2	3	4	5	6	7	8	9	10

The Forum is a waste of my time.

The Forum is an extremely
meaningful and important part
of my life.

Forum Review

The Forum Review is an in-depth view of Forum health, behaviors and practices. Many Forums use the results to prompt important discussions on Forum strengths and opportunities for improvement.

Objectives

- To assess member views of the Forum
- To raise awareness of Forum strengths and opportunities for improvement

Facilitator Info

Depth Level:	Medium
Facilitation Skills:	Medium
Estimated Time:	• 1 hour to complete the survey • 2 hours to compile the survey results • 2 hours to discuss survey results and identify actions
Tools Needed:	Flipchart, markers
Handouts:	Forum Review Survey form (4 pages, below)
Pre-work:	None
Notes:	• Ideally, this survey should be administered using an online survey tool and the results should be compiled before the retreat. At the retreat, the results can be discussed as a developmental exercise for the Forum. • Many Forums perform this survey annually and save the results in order to have an ongoing record of the Forum's health and life cycle.
Author/Source:	Joan Mara

Facilitator Instructions

1) Give each member a copy of the survey. Let everyone know if the survey is intended to be anonymous. (Usually, an anonymous survey inspires more candid replies.)
2) Collect the results and compile them before the Forum retreat.
3) At the retreat, lead the Forum in a discussion of the survey results. Focus on strengths and opportunities for improvement. Ideally, select three areas where the Forum would like to improve over the next year.

Forum Review Survey
Please take a few moments to respond to the following questions.

A) Forum Satisfaction
Please respond to the following questions by placing yourself on the continuum at the point that best reflects where you are right now.

1) Right now my level of commitment to the group is:

1	2	3	4	5	6	7	8	9	10
the lowest it has ever been				wavering				my level of commitment is high	

2) My level of enthusiasm, energy and creativity for moving the group forward is:

1	2	3	4	5	6	7	8	9	10
my batteries are dead (no energy)				enough enthusiasm & energy to get by				I am charged and ready to create the future	

3) Right now the value I'm receiving from being in the group is:

1	2	3	4	5	6	7	8	9	10
minimal				moderate				significant	

4) I'd rate the value I'm <u>generating</u> (through my participation) for others in the group as:

1	2	3	4	5	6	7	8	9	10
inconsistent, insignificant				moderately valuable				significantly helpful to other members	

5) When I think about how much risk I'm taking in the group right now I'd rate it as:

1	2	3	4	5	6	7	8	9	10
I'm taking fewer risks than ever				I take small risks occasionally				I'm still taking big risks in what I disclose here	

Forum Review Survey, continued

B) Nuts and Bolts (a.k.a. True Confessions)

Attendance/Punctuality

1) In the last year how often have you been late to a meeting? _____

2) "I've been late ____ times, and the Forum has collected _____ in late fees from me. Therefore, we

- do enforce the late penalty
- do not enforce the late penalty
- inconsistently enforce the late penalty

3) In the last year how often have you missed a meeting?

4) If you have missed more than two meetings, has the Forum enforced its ground rule around attendance expectations?

Confidentiality

1) I feel _____% confident in the ability of our Forum to maintain the confidentiality agreement.
2) I feel _____% confident that if confidentiality was breached in this Forum we would deal with it (talk about it) vs. not address it.

Business Conflicts

1) I do absolutely no business and have no business connections with any other member of the Forum.

_____ True _____ False

2) I have some minimal business connections with other Forum members

_____ True _____ False

If true, describe all business dealings with other Forum members no matter how minimal:

3) I have entered into a significant business relationship with another member of the Forum.

Presentations

1) How many presentations have you done in the last year? How many were done in total in the last year within the group?

2) Was your presentation topic of a business or personal nature?

3) What percentage of the presentations in the group have been business, what percentage personal and family?

4) How many presentations have been of a deep nature where you think someone showed vulnerability? Was yours of a deep nature? Did you feel you were taking a risk?

Forum Review Survey, continued

C) Looking Ahead

1) Our greatest strength as a group is:

2) Our biggest challenge is:

3) Something we don't talk about, but we should is:

4) The two most important things we can do as a group to move forward are:

a)

b)

5) The most important thing I could do to strengthen this Forum is:

6) The one thing I would like to see to strengthen our Forum, from each member (listed individually below) is:

Name	What I'd like to see

Category 4
Forum Team Building

Use these exercises to work on the Forum itself. Team-building exercises can help integrate new members and re-invigorate existing members. These exercises also help to define your Forum's culture and how people interact.

Refer to Part 1 of this book, Planning Your Retreat, for information on how to facilitate exercises. Time estimates for individual exercises are based on an 8-person Forum. Adjust the time estimates as needed to accommodate the size of your Forum.

Category 4 Exercises

forumsherpa

Trust Fall

The Trust Fall is a classic teambuilding exercise. It requires the person falling to let go of their fears and put their trust in their fellow Forum members. This is a metaphor for one of the key objectives of the Forum – to let ourselves be open and vulnerable and trust that our Forum members will help us.

Objectives

- To build trust in your fellow Forum members by putting your safety in their hands (literally)
- To experience an increased level of trust and bonding

Facilitator Info

Depth Level:	Light
Facilitation Skills:	Basic
Estimated Time:	30 minutes
Tools Needed:	A sturdy chair
Handouts:	None
Pre-work:	None
Notes:	Safety Alert! You should have at least 7 members in your Forum to attempt this exercises so that 3 people can be positioned on each side of the line.
Author/Source:	Unknown, adapted for Forum

Facilitator Instructions

1) Divide into two lines, facing each other.
2) Ask one person to leave the line and climb up on a chair that is positioned at the end of the line. Then, ask this person to fall backwards into the group and let the Forum members catch them from falling. [IMPORTANT: To avoid injury, be sure you have at least 3 people on each side of the line before attempting this exercise!]
3) Take turns falling backwards from the chair until everyone has had the opportunity to fall.
4) As a group, talk about the following questions:
   a. What did it feel like to fall backwards into the arms of the others?
   b. What does it feel like to be responsible for another person's physical well-being?
   c. What did you learn about trust in this exercise?
   d. What do we need to do as a group to trust each other?

Team Success Stories

Team Success Stories is an exercise that helps the Forum identify actionable steps to help build and maintain a strong sense of team spirit. Members reflect on prior experiences inside and outside of Forum that contributed or detracted from a strong team experience, then compile and action list to implement changes.

Objectives

- To share stories of team effectiveness
- To discuss methods of translating team success stories into Forum reality

Facilitator Info

Depth Level:	Light
Facilitation Skills:	Basic
Estimated Time:	1 hour
Tools Needed:	Flipchart, markers, paper, pens/pencils
Handouts:	None
Pre-work:	None
Notes:	• This activity generates considerable energy and a celebratory team mood. The key to success is to move from the stories of spirited team performance in the past to discovering the source of that spirit in their current Forum experience. • This is a good activity to do at the end of the day, before an evening of relaxation and fun.
Author/Source:	"Building Team Spirit", adapted for Forum

Facilitator Instructions

1) Ask Forum members to write out a true story of an outstanding team spirit that occurred with the Forum. It should be a time in the life of the Forum when the group felt potent, alive, full of spirit, fresh, vital and full of possibility. Tell the story using the journalistic method:
   a. Who
   b. What
   c. Where
   d. When
   e. Why
   f. How

Team Success Stories, continued

2) Next, ask Forum members to think of a time when they felt a strong team spirit with another group (outside the Forum). Write out this story too, using the journalistic method:
   a. Who
   b. What
   c. Where
   d. When
   e. Why
   f. How

3) Finally, ask everyone to think of a time (inside or outside of Forum) when team spirit was crushed. How and why did it happen? How could it have been avoided?

4) Allow 15 minutes for steps one, two and three.

5) Ask each person to share their stories. Before you begin, ask everyone to listen for underlying threads that exist in multiple stories. Write these threads on the flipchart on a page titled "Threads" and post the page on the wall. Allow about 30 minutes for storytelling.

6) On the next flipchart page, write "Actions/Ideas". Now, ask the team to consider what the Forum currently does, or could do, to generate this quality of spirit. Ask what action steps the Forum could take to reinforce and extend this sense of spirit, possibility and greatness. Record these ideas on the second flipchart page. Allow 10 minutes to generate action ideas.

7) Review the Threads and the Action Ideas and identify actionable changes the Forum will make. Record the decisions and assign accountability where appropriate.

Appreciating Diversity

The Appreciating Diversity exercise is an opportunity to reflect on diversity (or lack of diversity) within the Forum. The process prompts introspective thinking and builds awareness on diversity, exclusion and inclusion. People learn more about themselves and about each other.

Objectives

- To help Forum members appreciate the diversity of their membership, noticing the diversity represented and missing in the Forum
- To encourage Forum members to openly share their experiences and to celebrate the uniqueness and differences of Forum members

Facilitator Info

Depth Level:	Medium
Facilitation Skills:	Medium
Estimated Time:	1 hour
Tools Needed:	• No tools needed • Room setup – wide open space with no table or chairs in the way.
Handouts:	None
Pre-work:	None
Notes:	• This is a powerful activity for creating awareness of diversity operating within the Forum. • Don't rush or skip any parts of the activity. Merely allow the group to savor its diversity. • The strength of the activity is in the silence as members move from one side of the room to the other.
Author/Source:	"Building Team Spirit", adapted for Forum

Facilitator Instructions

1) Ask the entire Forum to stand together as a group at one end of the room. (If you are a member of this Forum, that includes you.)
2) Explain that the first part of this exercise will be done in silence and that participants will remain standing during this portion of the experience. Tell participants they will walk to the opposite end of the room each time you call out a category that "fits" or describes who they are.
3) Coach the team to notice who is with them and who is separated from them in each category, noticing the quality of spirit and how they feel about the categories that are mentioned.
4) As a category is identified that "fits" with Forum members, they should walk to the other end of the room, turn to those members who walked with them, and silently make eye contact with each member. These persons should then look back at their colleagues at the other end of the room, observing their own feelings, before returning back to the full team. (If you are a member of the Forum facilitating this exercise, you should participate in walking back and forth across the room.)

Appreciating Diversity, continued

5) For each category, provide the following instructions:
   a. "Please walk to the other side of the room if you are ..... (read the category)."
   b. Notice who is with you, and silently make eye contact with them.
   c. Notice who is not with you, looking back across the room.
   d. Notice the quality of the spirit that you feel.
   e. Please walk back to the full team.

6) Here are the categories of differences. "Please walk to the other side of the room if...
   - You are wearing the color red.
   - You are a sports fanatic.
   - You have brown eyes.
   - You have a parent who was a major influence on you.
   - You love being in nature.
   - You are a vegetarian.
   - You are an artist or performer.
   - You currently have a passion in your life.
   - You occasionally feel depressed.
   - You are a Native American or at least one of your parents is a Native American.
   - You are African American or of African descent.
   - You are Asian-American or Asian.
   - You are Latin American.
   - You are of mixed ancestry.
   - You are a woman.
   - You have worked in your current business for ten years or more.
   - You are over 45 years of age.
   - You are under 25 years of age.
   - You were raised in a family that was considered poor.
   - You were raised by a relative other than a parent, or you lived in an orphanage or foster home, for some part of your childhood.
   - You were raised in a faith that was different from most of the people around you.
   - You have worked in your current business for 20 years or more.
   - You have lost a brother, sister, mother or father to illness.
   - You were raised by a single parent.
   - You are currently a single parent.
   - You or a family member is lesbian, gay or bisexual.
   - You were raised in a farming community.
   - You were raised in the Jewish faith.
   - You are a Republican.
   - You have been dangerously sick.
   - You come from a family in which alcohol or drugs are a problem.
   - You were raised in the Catholic faith.
   - You or a member of your family has been considered mentally ill.
   - You were considered fat at any time in your life.
   - You were not able to fully experience your childhood as circumstances required that you act as an adult.
   - You have felt judged or belittled due to circumstances beyond your control (such as race, birthplace, family of origin, etc.)

7) Everyone can sit down now and the code of silence is over.

Appreciating Diversity, continued

Discussion Questions

8) Ask everyone to reflect on the implications of what they experienced.
   a. How did it feel to be part of the group walking across the room?
   b. How did it feel to be part of the group that stayed on the same side?
   c. How did it feel to be part of a larger group?
   d. How did it feel to be part of a smaller group?
   e. Was there a time when anyone felt embarrassed or uncomfortable?
   f. Was there a time when you felt proud to be on a particular side of the room?
   g. Was there a time when you wanted to say something to someone?
   h. How did you feel about this exercise?

Talking Stick

The Talking Stick exercise is an opportunity to connect with nature and connect with each other, using rich, symbolic imagery from Native American culture. People reflect on the value of Forum, then share their thoughts in a peaceful, outdoor setting.

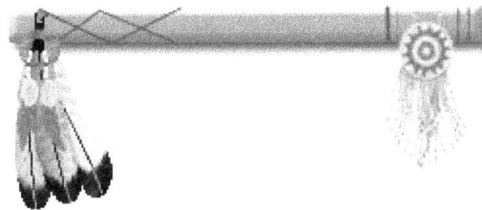

Objectives

- To explore ways that the Forum can increase value for its members
- To use a unique setting and a technique from Native American culture to enhance team members' ability to communicate with each other

Facilitator Info

Depth Level:	Medium
Facilitation Skills:	Medium
Estimated Time:	1 hour
Tools Needed:	• Talking stick – tree branch about 15" long and 1" thick, a feather, a piece of leather to tie the feather to the stick • Native American flute music • Herbal tea (optional)
Handouts:	None
Pre-work:	None
Notes:	This exercise can be done for other topics of importance to the Forum. For example, instead of using the word VALUE, you could insert a different word such as trust, commitment or love
Author/Source:	"Team Games for Trainers", adapted for Forum

Facilitator Instructions

1) Explain the objectives of the exercise. Identify the key word of the exercise – "VALUE". The exercise is focused on bringing value to the Forum.
2) In a comfortable, private outdoor setting, have Forum members sit in a circle on the ground. Play Native American flute music softly in the background. Optionally, serve herbal tea in large mugs to further underscore the connection to earth, the plant kingdom and water.
3) Ask everyone to close their eyes for several minutes and feel, hear and smell the nature around them.
4) Ask everyone to open their eyes and ground themselves in terms of six directions: north, south, east, west, sky, earth. Be sure everyone knows where the sun rises, its intended course across the sky, and where it sets relative to where they are sitting at this moment.
5) When everyone seems relaxed and "grounded", explain the Talking Stick. The person who holds the Talking Stick is the only person who can talk. Each person should hold the stick for up to 3 minutes and feel free to say whatever is on their mind. Ideally, people should share comments about value in the Forum – value they have received in the past, value they hope to receive in the future, ways the Forum provides value to its members, ways that the Forum could offer even more value to its members.

Talking Stick, continued

6) When the person finishes what they want to say, they should finish by saying the single word: "VALUE".

7) Then they will pass the talking stick to the next person.

8) Pass the stick on if you have nothing to say. It's okay to have nothing to say. You will have another chance.

9) Continue passing the stick around from person to person, encouraging those who didn't speak the previous time around the circle. Continue as long as anyone has anything to say.

Debrief Questions

a) What are the tangible changes the Forum can make to increase value for its members?

b) This type of exercise can be uncomfortable for some people. Did anyone feel uncomfortable? Did their discomfort affect the exercise? If so, how?

Listening Skills

Listening Skills is an exercise that enables Forum members to analyze their own listening habits. Twenty behaviors are identified for people to self-assess their strengths and weaknesses in terms of listening. Forum members then select three areas of weakness that they would like to improve.

Objectives

- To build awareness of your listening habits
- To learn more about your fellow Forum members
- To self-identify areas for improvement

Facilitator Info

Depth Level:	Light
Facilitation Skills:	Basic
Estimated Time:	30 minutes
Tools Needed:	None
Handouts:	Listening Skills worksheet (next page)
Pre-work:	None
Notes:	None
Author/Source:	Ellie Byrd

Facilitator Instructions

1) Read the following paragraphs on listening skills.

> Many people do not listen effectively, even though it is one of the most critical skills in organizations and in relationships. Poor listening habits can lead to numerous misunderstandings and conflicts. By focusing our attention on listening, we can increase retention and become better communicators.
>
> An ancient Greek philosopher said "We have **two ears** and **one mouth** so that we can listen twice as much as we speak."

2) Distribute copies of the Listening Skills worksheet to all members.
3) Ask everyone to write ALWAYS, SOMETIMES or NEVER to the left of each item to indicate how the statement describes them. Allow 15 minutes for this portion of the exercise.
4) After everyone has marked all of the items, ask them to circle any specific items where they feel they could improve their listening skills.
5) Ask each person to share three changes they would like to make in their listening habits. People are welcome to ask the Forum to help them make these changes. For example, if someone interrupts frequently, they could ask the Forum to "police" them and let them know when they are interrupting.

Listening Skills Worksheet

Read each sentence. Write the word ALWAYS, SOMETIMES or NEVER in the blank to identify how well the sentence describes your listening behavior.

A. _____ While someone is talking, I try to hear other conversations around me to keep up with what's going on.

B. _____ I prefer that someone just present the facts and skip the opinions so I can draw my own conclusions.

C. _____ I think ahead and prepare my response while the other person is talking.

D. _____ As someone is speaking to me, I avoid eye contact. I'm not particularly interested in non-verbal cues such as facial expressions and body language.

E. _____ If I hear something I think is wrong, I'll interrupt immediately to explain why I disagree.

F. _____ When I find myself not listening to someone, I will pretend to pay attention to what he or she is saying.

G. _____ I start to judge the merit of what someone says from the very first sentence.

H. _____ I prefer to communicate through email or text so that I don't have to deal with idle chit chat.

I. _____ I anticipate what people will say next as they are speaking.

J. _____ I show my reactions on my face to what people are saying to let them know right away whether or not I agree.

K. _____ When a person is talking to me, I am ready immediately with a response as soon as they stop.

L. _____ A person's appearance is important to me in deciding whether or not to listen attentively to what that individual says.

M. _____ If I'm not sure what someone means, I will ask for clarification before he or she has continued talking much longer.

N. _____ A speaker needs to present the information in a lively and entertaining way to keep my interest.

O. _____ I have biases and opinions which affect my ability or willingness to listen to what some people have to say.

- How many items did you mark as ALWAYS _____ SOMETIMES _____ NEVER _____

- Identify the top three listening skills that you would like to improve:

  1) _____

  2) _____

  3) _____

Annual Forum Planning

Annual Forum Planning is an exercise that enables Forums to proactively develop a plan for the coming year. This is particularly useful when the role of Moderator changes at the annual retreat. The Forum can discuss and find alignment on a variety of areas: Forum Goals, Forum Roles, Forum Norms, Meeting Calendar and Individual Goals.

Objectives
- To help your Forum prepare for the year
- To establish a cohesive direction and gain support from all members
- To build alignment and purpose within the Forum

Facilitator Info

Depth Level:	Medium
Facilitation Skills:	Medium
Estimated Time:	3 hours
Tools Needed:	Flipchart, markers, masking tape
Handouts:	<ul><li>Annual Forum Roles worksheet</li><li>Annual Forum Calendar worksheet</li><li>Annual Individual Goals worksheet</li></ul>
Pre-work:	<ul><li>Read the Forum Norms (Constitution) and make note of any changes you would like to discuss.</li><li>Update your calendar with upcoming events (holidays, kids' events, vacations, etc.) so that the next year of meeting dates can be selected.</li></ul>
Notes:	Facilitation skills are important in this exercise. You are leading the discussion, but you must achieve a balance of letting members express their opinions without mayhem breaking out. You are a member too, so your own feelings need to be included without dominating the discussion.
Author/Source:	Ellie Byrd

Facilitator Instructions

1) Begin with the Annual Forum Goals. This will establish alignment and set the tone for what is ahead in the coming year.
   a. Ask Forum members to make suggestions of annual goals for the group. Write each suggestion on a flipchart. Use multiple sheets of flipchart paper and tape them on the wall. Remember that no suggestion is silly or stupid or wrong. Every suggestion must be written down. Examples of Forum goals are: all members meet with each other member one-on-one during the year, all members attend a learning event together, no members lost, increase punctuality, decrease absences, improve survey measurements, cumulative 10% revenue increase for members, etc.
   b. Ask Forum members to vote for their top 3 favorite goals by giving them a marker and asking them to place a checkmark by each one.
   c. Take the top five to seven goals and re-write them on another sheet of flipchart paper.
   d. Again, ask all Forum members to vote for their top 3 favorite goals.
   e. The 3 goals receiving the most votes become the Forum's annual goals.

Annual Forum Planning, continued

2) Proceed to the Annual Forum Roles worksheet. First, determine which roles the Forum would like to assign. List the tasks that the person will do for each role. Then, ask for volunteers for each role. Attempt to get volunteers for roles rather than assigning roles to people. (Buy-in tends to be higher if the person has volunteered for the role!) Examples of Forum roles are: Moderator Elect, Treasurer, Parking Lot Attendant, Retreat Planner(s), Social Chair, Technology Chair, Chapter Board Representative, etc.

3) Continue to the Annual Forum Calendar worksheet. Start with the first column – date and time. Complete these for the year before moving on to the remaining columns. Note that some Forums assign presenters for the entire year in advance at the same time the calendar is set. After all columns are complete, discuss the process for rescheduling a meeting and write it down.

4) Next, ask members to complete the Annual Individual Goals. These can be business, family or personal. (Optionally, this can be distributed in advance so that people can come to the session with their goals prepared.) Ask each person to share their goals and have someone compile them on a master list. Return to the annual calendar and select the frequency (monthly, quarterly) when annual goal progress will be reviewed.

5) Finally, ask each member to look at your Forum Norms (Constitution). Preferably, this is distributed in advance so that people can read it and make notes before the session. Ask one person to take the role of master scribe and write down all changes to the Norms. Then, review the entire document, or ask people to bring up items they would like to discuss. After you have discussed all items in question, review the changes or decisions and close the exercise.

6) Before your next regular Forum meeting, ask the master scribe to make all edits and email the revised Forum Norms (Constitution) to everyone. At your next meeting, vote on acceptance of the revised document. Note that sticking points can be discussed at the next meeting again.

Annual Forum Roles

Assigning annual Forum roles serves several purposes.

1) It gets all members actively involved in the running of the Forum.
2) It alleviates the heavy burden on the Moderator to manage everything themselves.
3) It helps to keep the Forum running smoothly.
4) It helps avoid things "slipping through the cracks".

Determine the roles you would like to assign. Try to have as many roles as you have members in your Forum.

Ask each Forum member to volunteer for a role. Alternatively, the Moderator can assign roles.

Annual Forum Planning, continued

Annual Roles Worksheet

Role	Description / Tasks	Name

Annual Forum Planning, continued

Annual Calendar Worksheet

Establishing a full year calendar generally helps everyone to plan more effectively.

If your Forum is uncomfortable setting dates 12 months in advance, strive for a 6-month calendar, then add one more month to the end at each monthly meeting.

Annual Forum Meeting Calendar

Date, Time	Host	Location	Presenter & Coach*
Jan			
Feb			
Mar			
Apr			
May			
Jun			
Jul			
Aug			
Sep			
Oct			
Nov			
Dec			

*Some Forums assign presenters in advance while others draw from the Parking Lot. Use this column at your discretion.

Defined Process for Rescheduling a Meeting:

_____

_____

_____

Annual Forum Planning, continued

Annual Individual Goals Worksheet

The primary objective of setting individual goals is to help Forum members focus on their objectives, to encourage members to help each other achieve their goals, and to provide a level of accountability within the Forum group.

1) Have each member compile a list of up to three goals in each of several categories. Note that the categories may vary for different people – Business, Personal, Family, Community, Spiritual, etc. Attempt to make all goals SMART*.
2) Have each member share their goals with the Forum group. Allow five minutes per person.
3) Determine a schedule of how often the goals will be reviewed and progress reported. Usually, this will be a quarterly review. Add the review reminder to your Annual Calendar.

My Individual Goals

Business	1. 2. 3.
Family	1. 2. 3.
Personal	1. 2. 3.
Other? _____	1. 2. 3.

*SMART Goals
S = specific
M = measurable
A = aligned (with my vision and values)
R = realistic
T = timed

Stop, Start, Continue (Green Tail)

Stop, Start, Continue is an exercise that enables Forum members to provide feedback to each other about their contribution, action and behaviors in Forum. The exercise offers an opportunity for people to voice thoughts that they may have been suppressing. By the end of the exercise, everyone has offered input to everyone else and received input from everyone in the Forum.

Objectives

- To share our thoughts and feelings about how members contribute to the Forum experience
- To gain input and insight from our fellow Forum members on our own contribution to the Forum

Facilitator Info

Depth Level:	Medium
Facilitation Skills:	Advanced
Estimated Time:	45 minutes
Tools Needed:	A large stack of 3x5 cards, pens/pencils
Handouts:	None
Pre-work:	None
Notes:	• This exercise is a good tool for allowing members to vent frustrations in a non-confrontational manner. It can help to clear the air when there are interpersonal relationship issues. • This can be an uncomfortable exercise for some people. • Remind everyone to focus on the behavior as the problem, not the person. • If your Forum is experiencing extreme difficulties, you may want to consider bringing in a professional facilitator to work through this exercise. • This exercise can be used for other types of input, such as business, health or communication skills.
Author/Source:	Unknown, adapted for Forum

Facilitator Instructions

1) Each member gets a blank 3 x 5 card for every other member of the Forum. Write each person's name on a card until you have a card for every Forum member. Do NOT write your own name on the cards.
2) On each card, write Stop, Start and Continue. Then write down one thing you would like that member to stop doing, one thing you would like them to start doing, and one thing you would like them to continue doing in Forum.
3) Complete one card for each member of the Forum.
4) After everyone has completed all of the cards, collect the cards and sort them by person. Distribute the cards directly to each person. When finished, you will have a stack of cards in front of you from your fellow Forum members with suggestions on things you should stop, start and continue doing.

Stop, Start, Continue (Green Tail), continued

5) Allow each person time to read through their cards on their own. Note the "green tail" syndrome.

The Green Tail Syndrome

If one person tells you that you have a green tail, they are crazy. If two people tell you that you have a green tail, it's a conspiracy. But if three people tell you that you have a green tail, you turn around and look.

The implication here is that if several of your Forum members say that you are exhibiting a particular behavior, there is likely to be validation in the repetition. It may be a matter of perception, in other words, they perceive the behavior whether you intend it to be so or not. It may also be a matter of awareness in that we are often unaware of how our behavior may be affecting others.

---

6) Go around the room one at a time and let each member share anything they learned from their cards. This should be done in a non-judgmental manner. In other words, if someone is not comfortable talking about their "green tail", they shouldn't be forced into it.

7) Encourage members to talk with the Moderator privately if they have concerns about any of their cards.

Our Featured Forum

Our Featured Forum is a visualization exercise whereby the group constructs an article for a local news source on the Forum experience. Discussing the objectives, structure and take-away value of the Forum brings clarity to the group and it often sparks valuable conversations.

Objectives

- To assess the Forum's strengths and the value it brings to the members
- To give Forum members an opportunity to share how the Forum has helped them

Facilitator Info

Depth Level:	Light
Facilitation Skills:	Basic
Estimated Time:	30 minutes
Tools Needed:	Flipchart, markers
Handouts:	None
Pre-work:	None
Notes:	For a variation and even more impact, break up into small teams and write different segments of the article. Then come back together and compose the entire article. Consider submitting it to a local business magazine with a picture of your Forum on retreat. You may get some free publicity! (Allow at least 1 hour for this variation.)
Author/Source:	Ellie Byrd

Facilitator Instructions

Congratulations! You have just learned that your Forum will be profiled in an important business magazine! The editor assigned to your story has asked for your Forum members to provide an outline for the article.

1) Explain the objective of the exercise.
2) Consider the following questions:
   a. What is the Forum?
   b. What makes it unique?
   c. How does it function?
   d. What makes it a valuable experience?
   e. How does the Forum support its members?
   f. etc.
3) Develop your outline on the flipchart with input from everyone. Be sure you include all the points that you hope the article will cover.
4) When you have finished the outline, compare this ideal view of the Forum to the actual reality. Is there a difference? If so, how can the Forum move toward the ideal? Brainstorm on how to do this.

Forum SWOT Analysis

Using the traditional SWOT Analysis model, the Forum engages in a lively discussion on the health, value and operations of the Forum.

Objectives

- To assess the Forum's strengths, weaknesses, opportunities and threats in a traditional SWOT analysis format
- To gain clarity on how the Forum is doing, the risks it may be facing and how to proactively avoid potential problems
- To build awareness and initiate meaningful conversations on the Forum's overall health

Facilitator Info

Depth Level:	Light
Facilitation Skills:	Medium
Estimated Time:	1 hour
Tools Needed:	Flipchart, markers
Handouts:	None
Pre-work:	None
Notes:	As a variation, start the exercise by asking each member to create a SWOT analysis for their own business. Share the results with each other to learn more about each other's businesses and get into the solution frame of mind.
Author/Source:	Ellie Byrd

Facilitator Instructions

1) Explain the objective of the exercise.
2) On the flipchart, draw the traditional SWOT analysis grid. Be sure that everyone understands that Strengths and Weaknesses are internal; Opportunities and Threats are external.

Forum SWOT Analysis, continued

	Helpful To achieving the objective	Harmful To achieving the objective
Internal Attributes of the company	Strengths	Weaknesses
External Attributes of the environment	Opportunities	Threats

3) Divide the Forum into two groups. One group is tasked with identifying Strengths and Weaknesses. The other group is to identify Opportunities and Threats. Allow 10 minutes for this.

4) Bring Forum members back together and let each group share the points they identified, writing them up on the flipchart. Allow time for some free form discussion, additions and changes as each group presents their ideas. Seek to achieve consensus in each of the four areas.

5) When the group feels that the SWOT analysis is complete, have a discussion on how the Forum can proactively work to reduce weaknesses and threats. Select three weaknesses and/or threats that the Forum would like to work on over the next year. Scribe ideas on a flipchart and make note of any action items the group agrees to embrace.

Three Little Pigs

The Forum engages in a fun competition to re-write the traditional tale of the "Three Little Pigs" from the wolf's point of view. The intent of the exercise is to build awareness around different perspectives by learning NOT to jump to conclusions too quickly.

Objectives

- To help Forum members appreciate that there are two sides to every story
- To learn to be more understanding of situations, personalities and backgrounds
- To be creative and have fun

Facilitator Info

Depth Level:	Light
Facilitation Skills:	Basic
Estimated Time:	30 minutes
Tools Needed:	A copy of the children's fairy tale - "The Three Little Pigs"
Handouts:	None
Pre-work:	None
Notes:	This exercise can be helpful for a Forum that is working on diversity or judgment issues.
Author/Source:	Unknown, adapted for Forum

Facilitator Instructions

1) Explain the objective of the exercise.
2) Ask someone to recount the children's story of the Three Little Pigs.
3) At the end of the story, divide the Forum into two groups.
4) Ask each group to go somewhere (outside the room, on their own) for 20 minutes and come up with another version of the Three Little Pigs story. The new version needs to be from the wolf's perspective and it needs to perfectly explain and defend the wolf's actions as understandable. For example, perhaps the wolf simply had a bad cold and a powerful sneeze. Who could blame him for eating the pigs that died when their houses fell down as a result of his sneezing?
5) When the Forum groups return, have them share their respective stories. (These are usually hilarious!)

Debrief Questions

a) Ask individuals to think of a case where they have had an impression of someone and later found out that their impression was wrong. Describe the situation.
b) Engage in an open discussion of different personality types and how we can misread people, especially people with different backgrounds or cultures.

Category 5

Building Team Spirit, Fun

Use these exercises to challenge individuals to solve problems as a group. These exercises will require the strengths of both practical and creative personalities. The team must weigh options and make choices that affect the outcome of the project in a relatively short time frame. Everyone has different skills and styles, but people still have to find ways to work together, reach consensus and build productive relationships. Building on each others' strengths makes the whole team stronger.

Refer to Part 1 of this book, Planning Your Retreat, for information on how to facilitate exercises. Time estimates for individual exercises are based on an 8-person Forum. Adjust the time estimates as needed to accommodate the size of your Forum.

Category 5 Exercises

forumsherpa

Time Capsule

The Time Capsule exercise is an opportunity for the Forum to talk about the purpose and culture of the group in a fun, creative manner.

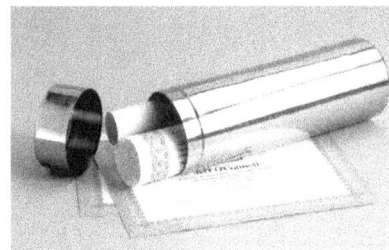

Objectives

- To discuss the purpose and culture of the Forum
- To select objects and ideas that represent your Forum's culture that could go into a time capsule

Facilitator Info

Depth Level:	Light
Facilitation Skills:	Basic
Estimated Time:	1 hour
Tools Needed:	Flipchart, markers, pencils
Handouts:	Time Capsule Worksheet
Pre-work:	None
Notes:	None
Author/Source:	"All Together Now", adapted for Forum

Facilitator Instructions

1) Explain that the Forum has the opportunity to prepare a time capsule that will be placed in a safe deposit box with instructions that it is not to be opened for one hundred years. The Forum members need to collectively decide what will be placed in the time capsule, and the items must represent the present culture of the Forum.
2) First, identify the three items. Allow 5 minutes to talk through this. Write the three items on the flipchart.
3) Distribute a copy of the Time Capsule Worksheet to each member. Ask each person, on their own, to write a personal statement about each of the three items that would provide a stranger with an accurate picture of the Forum's culture. Each statement must be 25 words or less. Allow 10 minutes to work on this.
4) As a group, discuss the individual statements and work together to produce a single statement for the entire group for each of the three items. Allow 20 minutes to work on this.
5) Write the final three statements on the flipchart.
6) Answer the following discussion questions:
   a. How difficult was it for the team to select the three items?
   b. Does the information in the time capsule accurately represent your personal view of your Forum's culture? In what way? Why or why not?
   c. Were the individual descriptions easy or difficult to articulate?
   d. How did the team approach the task of integrating the individual descriptions into a single, cohesive statement?
   e. Overall, did conflicts arise in the course of completing the task? How were these resolved?

Time Capsule Worksheet

Three items: 1. _____
              2. _____
              3. _____

My description of the three items (25 words or less):

Item #1:
Item #2:
Item #3:

Forum's collective description of the three items (25 words or less):

Item #1:
Item #2:
Item #3:

Wishful Thinking

Wishful Thinking is a guided exercise that helps the Forum think proactively and out-of-the-box on how the Forum can improve its teamwork.

Objectives

- To identify ways that the Forum can improve the team's ability to work together
- To discuss opportunities for improving communications, efficiency and accountability

Facilitator Info

Depth Level:	Light
Facilitation Skills:	Medium
Estimated Time:	30 minutes
Tools Needed:	Flipchart, markers, pencils
Handouts:	Wishful Thinking Slips (3 slips per person)
Pre-work:	None
Notes:	Let the decision-making process happen naturally.
Author/Source:	"All Together Now", adapted for Forum

Facilitator Instructions

1) Distribute 3 Wishful Thinking Slips to each person.
2) Explain that the Forum will be visited today by a special genie who can grant three wishes to help improve the Forum's ability to work together. In preparation for the genie's appearance, each Forum member is to write one wish on each of the three slips of paper. Allow 5 minutes for this.
3) When completed, each slip is folded in half and placed in a jar, bowl or paper bag.
4) Now the Forum is tasked with identifying three wishes that the group would like to see come true in respect to improved teamwork. The facilitator starts by reading the collected wish list slips. Then, facilitate a discussion to select the three wishes. Allow 15 minutes for this discussion.
5) Write the final three wishes on the flipchart.
6) Discuss the following debrief questions:
   a. How difficult was it to reach consensus on the three wishes for the final list?
   b. What type of decision-making process did the group use?
   c. How did the members of the Forum interact during the decision-making process?
      i. Was the discussion inclusive? Did everyone contribute?
      ii. Were there any natural leaders in the process? Did anyone dominate the conversation?
      iii. Did everyone have an opportunity to voice their opinion?
      iv. Was everyone in unanimous agreement? If not, how was consensus reached?
   d. How could the Forum make some of these wishes come true?
   e. Create an action list of next steps that can help the Forum implement the wishes.

Wishful Thinking Strips

Make enough copies of this page to have three strips per person. Use scissors to cut the page into individual strips.

I wish…

I wish…

I wish…

I wish…

I wish…

I wish…

I wish…

Human Spider Web

The Human Spider Web is a fun, physical exercise that tasks Forum members with untangling themselves from a random, spaghetti-like, interlaced mesh.

Objectives

- To loosen up, have fun, break down inhibitions
- To provide an opportunity to participate in a team and explore the dimensions of teamwork
- To observe teamwork, leadership, and problem solving skills

Facilitator Info

Depth Level:	Light
Facilitation Skills:	Basic
Estimated Time:	15 minutes
Tools Needed:	None
Handouts:	None
Pre-work:	None
Notes:	• This exercise must be done with an even number of participants. Six or eight people is optimum. • It's best if people are timed (as a way to increase the pressure). • Another alternative is to compete with another Forum (same number of people) to see which group finishes the task first. • When untangled, every other person will be facing backwards.
Author/Source:	Unknown, adapted for Forum

Facilitator Instructions

1) This exercise only works in a group of 6 or more people, with an even number of people. If you have an odd number of people, the extra person can take pictures!
2) Instruct members of the group to extend their left hand across the circle and grasp the left hand of the member who is approximately opposite them.
3) Next, have them extend their right hand across the circle and grasp the right hand of another individual (not the same person).
4) Inform them that their task is to unravel the spider web of interlocking arms without letting go of anyone's hands.

Discussion Questions

1) What was your first thought when you heard the nature of the task? (usually: "This will be impossible!")
2) What member behaviors detracted (or could detract) from the group's success in achieving its goal?
3) What lessons does this exercise have for future team building?

Embarrassing Moments

Embarrassing Moments is a fun game that exercises everyone's ability to think quickly on their feet and be creative. Be prepared to laugh!

Objectives

- To get to know each other better
- To have a good laugh

Facilitator Info

Depth Level:	Medium
Facilitation Skills:	Light
Estimated Time:	2 hours (great to do over a long, slow dinner)
Tools Needed:	Paper, pens/pencils
Handouts:	None
Pre-work:	None
Notes:	• This exercise is great to do over a long, slow dinner. (David's Forum had a long dinner of cheese fondue, followed by main course, followed by chocolate fondue, and plenty of wine! He says it's the only successful exercise they've ever done over dinner, and it was a blast!) • Assign a game coordinator or a timekeeper because the fake stories can stretch pretty long – especially if alcohol is involved!
Author/Source:	David Ryan

Facilitator Instructions

1) Give each person a slip of paper and a pencil. Ask everyone to think of an embarrassing moment in their life. Then, think of three words that are associated with their embarrassing moment in some way. Here are some examples:
   a. football, sunglasses, dishwasher
   b. bunk beds, camera, brother
   c. fence, cow, salt shaker
   d. trumpet, bra, rabbit
2) Have everyone write down their three words, fold the paper and drop it in a basket.
3) Pick out a piece of paper and read the three words. Everybody at the table has to make up a story as if it was their story. The individual whose story is picked has to play along and tell their real story when it's their turn, without letting on that it's REALLY their story.
4) A vote is cast by each member at the end of each round to pick who they thought told the real story (don't reveal the truth yet!).
5) Continue the process until all the papers have been drawn, all the stories have been told and everyone has voted on who they think was the REAL storyteller for each one.
6) At the end, everyone confesses which story was really theirs.

Egg Drop

The Egg Drop competition is a fun opportunity for the Forum to work together in teams to achieve a competitive objective. Each group is provided with a collection of supplies and tasked with constructing a contraption that will protect a raw egg when dropped from a 2-story height.

Objective

- For Forums to engage in a fun, competitive activity and build team spirit

Facilitator Info

Depth Level:	Light
Facilitation Skills:	Basic
Estimated Time:	1 hour
Tools Needed:	For each group, provide the following: • 1 raw egg • 50 drinking straws • masking tape • six feet of string • chewing gum • scissors • cotton balls • lunch sack (small, brown paper bag) • drinking cup • 3 balloons • 2 lb. weight
Handouts:	None
Pre-work:	None
Notes:	• Select a "drop" location that is at least 2 stories high. • If multiple Forums are on retreat together, let entire Forums work together as a group and give out awards to the winning Forum. • See Egg Drop – Version 2 below for a variation on the standard Egg Drop Competition.
Author/Source:	Unknown, adapted for Forum

Facilitator Instructions

1) Explain the competition objective and the rules of the competition:
   a. The Forum will be divided into two groups.
   b. The goal is to drop a raw egg, without breaking it, from a designated location at least two stories high.
   c. Each group will have 45 minutes to develop and build an egg protection device with the supplies provided.

Egg Drop, continued

    d. The egg protection device can contain any combination of the materials provided. The egg and the 2 lb weight must be included in the design, but the other materials are all optional.

    e. One person will present a 3-minute speech to market your device to the larger group. This marketing time provides an "egg-cellent" opportunity to share the features and benefits of your design and why you feel your egg won't break when dropped.

    f. One person will drop the egg from a designated area.

2) Split the Forum into two groups and provide each group with a workspace and all supplies. Try to keep the workspaces far enough apart that teams can't hear each other or spy on each other's engineering ideas.

3) While constructing the contraption, the team must also develop a marketing pitch to promote their device and explain its benefits.

4) After the allotted development time, call the groups back together and let the competition begin!

5) If possible, assign an impartial judge to rate the marketing presentations and to officiate on whether the eggs survived.

6) The criteria for a winning team is to design a device that protects the egg from breaking. A second prize will be awarded to the most creative marketing presentation.

Egg Drop – Version 2

The Challenge: Protect a raw egg so it won't break when it's dropped six feet to the floor.

The Rules: Use only the materials provided, keep one-third of the egg showing, complete your project in 20 minutes or less, listen to everyone's ideas and have fun!

The Materials for each team:
- one raw egg
- one six-inch, round, plastic foam plate
- two chopsticks
- two jumbo paper clips
- two large rubber bands
- two 18-inch pieces of string
- two toilet paper tubes
- one sheet of gummed file folder labels
- one 12-inch plastic bag

The Test: After each team has created its contraption, appoint one representative to come forward, hold the egg six feet off the ground and drop it onto a carpeted area (covered with a large trash bag).

One hint: Parachute models abound, but other ideas work, too.

Mystery Recipe

Test your culinary skills in this fun, creative exercise. The Forum is provided with a list of ingredients but no recipe, then tasked with creating an edible desert.

Objectives

- To work together as a team to cook something delicious
- To have fun

Facilitator Info

Depth Level:	Light
Facilitation Skills:	Basic
Estimated Time:	1 hour
Tools Needed:	Ingredients and supplies listed below
Handouts:	None
Pre-work:	None
Notes:	This exercise only works when you have free access to a kitchen (hint: the recipe is an apple crumb pie with ice cream)
Author/Source:	Ellie Byrd

Facilitator Instructions

The Forum is given the ingredients to make a dessert, but no recipe! Note that every ingredient will be eaten with the dessert but is not necessarily cooked IN the dessert. The Forum must work together to figure out what they are going to make and how they are going to make it. This exercise will require everyone to work together as a team toward a common goal.

Ingredients	Supplies
1¼ c. graham cracker crumbs	medium mixing bowl
3 T. sugar	mixing spoon
¼ c. melted butter	measuring cup
6 medium cooking apples – peeled, cored and sliced	measuring spoons
2 T. flour	9" pie plate
2 T. butter	knife
½ c. sugar	serving bowls
¼ c. brown sugar	utensils
½ t. cinnamon	
1 t. lemon juice	
¼ t. nutmeg	
¼ t. salt	
ice cream	

At the conclusion of the exercise, everyone can eat the dessert! (... unless there has been a catastrophe in the kitchen!)

Gum Drop Tower

The Gum Drop Tower exercise engages the Forum in a fun activity that requires good teamwork and smart engineering. A unique twist of this exercise is that the teams cannot speak while they are contructing their tower.

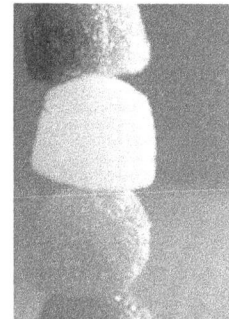

Objectives

- To engage in a fun, competitive activity
- To build team spirit
- To explore alternate means of communications – other than talking

Facilitator Info

Depth Level:	Light
Facilitation Skills:	Basic
Estimated Time:	30 minutes
Tools Needed:	For each group, provide the following: • A package of gumdrops • A box of matches • A cup of uncooked macaroni
Handouts:	None
Pre-work:	None
Notes:	• Provide each team with a private work area to construct their tower. • If multiple Forums are on retreat together, let entire Forums work together as a group and give out awards to the winning Forum.
Author/Source:	Unknown, adapted for Forum

Facilitator Instructions

1) Explain the objective and the rules of the competition:
   a. The Forum will be divided into two groups.
   b. The goal is to build the highest tower that can stand up without human help.
   c. Very important – people cannot speak or whisper or write during the exercise!
2) Split the Forum into two groups and provide each group with a workspace and supplies. Try to keep the workspaces far enough apart that they can't spy on each other's engineering ideas.
3) Give the groups 5 minutes to construct their tower.
4) After the towers are constructed, answer the following questions together:
   a. How well did the group work together?
   b. What was each person's role in the group?
   c. What was most frustrating about the exercise?
   d. How could the group improve their interaction if they were to repeat the exercise?
5) Optionally, mix up the teams and repeat the exercise. What changed the second time?

Square Rope

The Square Rope exercise tasks Forum members to work together on a competitive mission while blindfolded.

Objectives

- To engage in a fun, competitive activity and build team spirit
- To experience how we communicate when we are visually impaired

Facilitator Info

Depth Level:	Light
Facilitation Skills:	Basic
Estimated Time:	30 minutes
Tools Needed:	For each group, provide the following: • Blindfolds (one for each Forum member) • Two 20m (approximately 65 feet) long ropes
Handouts:	None
Pre-work:	None
Notes:	If multiple Forums are on retreat together, let entire Forums work together as a group and give out awards to the winning Forum.
Author/Source:	Unknown, adapted for Forum

Facilitator Instructions

1) Explain the competition objectives and the rules of the game:
   a. The Forum will be divided into two groups.
   b. The goal is to take a 20m (65 ft) long rope and make it into a square of 5m (6 ft) length sides.
   c. Members can talk to each other, but they can't see. Everyone is blindfolded!
2) Split the Forum into two groups. Blindfold everyone, then give each group their rope.
3) After the squares are formed, remove the blindfolds and answer the following debrief questions together.

Debrief Questions

a) How square are the squares?
b) How well did the group work together?
c) What was each person's role in the group?
d) What was most frustrating about the exercise?
e) How could the group improve their interaction if they were to repeat the exercise?

Pictorial Scavenger Hunt

The Pictorial Scavenger Hunt is an opportunity for the Forum to actively explore the retreat area/city and take a series of specific photographs in the prescribed time limit.

Objectives

- To engage in a fun, competitive activity
- To build team spirit

Facilitator Info

Depth Level:	Light
Facilitation Skills:	Basic
Estimated Time:	1½ hours
Tools Needed:	A digital camera or cell phone
Handouts:	List of Pictures (see below)
Pre-work:	None
Notes:	• Feel free to vary this exercise to make it more specific to the location where you are holding your retreat. • If multiple Forums are on retreat together, let entire Forums work together as a group and give out awards to the winning Forum.
Author/Source:	Ellie Byrd

Facilitator Instructions

1) Explain the objective and the rules of the competition:
   a. The Forum will be divided into two groups.
   b. Each group will have a list of 12 pictures that they are to take.
   c. The group that gets all the pictures in the least amount of time wins!
2) Split the Forum into two groups. Give them their list of pictures (below).
3) Start the timer and let the fun begin!
4) After both groups have completed their pictures, create a slide show to share the pictures.
5) As a Forum, discuss the following questions together:
   a. How well did the group work together?
   b. What was each person's role in the group?
   c. How could the group improve their interaction if they were to repeat the exercise?

Pictorial Scavenger Hunt, continued

List of Pictures
1) A picture of a living, breathing (non-human) animal
2) A picture of one of your Forum members standing on their head
3) A picture that includes an electrical device that the entire group is using
4) A picture that includes the following 3 primary colors – red, blue and yellow
5) A picture of a tree from a position of lying down on the ground below it
6) A picture of the other team – when they don't know you've gotten their picture!
7) A picture of an historical artifact. This could be a statue, antique, picture, etc. of historical significance
8) A picture of your entire group, with everyone making a funny face
9) A picture of two things that are opposites
10) A picture of something edible
11) A picture of something that is completely handmade
12) A selfie picture

Scavenger Hunt Variation
(submitted by Nancy Leach, Nashville)

"One of the people in our Forum developed a scavenger hunt for the small town where we had our retreat. We split into 2 teams and each team had to get 10 specific pictures. You had to photograph you/your team at places like: a bed in the local hospital, a jail cell, eating a pickled egg at the local VFW, on a boat, etc. It was a lot of fun and something that could be done in any climate. You do need someone who is familiar with the local area to prepare the list and make it fun."

Creativity

Creativity helps Forum members develop creative new ideas in a team setting. They will be able to think about how creativity plays a role in their lives as entrepreneurs.

Objectives

- To explore our creativity and think outside of the box
- To engage in a fun, creative, competitive activity

Facilitator Info

Depth Level:	Light
Facilitation Skills:	Basic
Estimated Time:	1 hour
Tools Needed:	Paper, pencils, flipchart, markers
Handouts:	None
Pre-work:	None
Notes:	None
Author/Source:	Unknown, adapted for Forum

Facilitator Instructions

1) Explain the objectives of the exercise.
2) To start the creative juices flowing, ask each member of the Forum to share the most recent creative idea they have had. Each person answers these two questions:
   a. What was the idea and how long ago did they have it (yesterday, last week, last month, etc.).
   b. What motivates you to be creative?
3) Next, read the following scenario to the Forum.

> Your Production Manager calls you in a panic – he's just realized that he accidentally overproduced one hundred thousand ball bearings! Your company can't afford the loss, but the mistake can't be undone! How can you use all the ball bearings for profit? Can you create a new product? What other types of ideas do you have?

4) Next, split the Forum into two groups. Give each group 15 minutes to come up with ideas. Here are some examples to get you started:
   - use them as jewelry
   - sew them into the bottom hem of curtains to weigh them down.
   - use them to stuff display furniture – the furniture will be too heavy to be stolen.
5) Come back together and ask each group to present their ideas.
6) As a group, discuss the following:
   a. How many identical ideas did the groups have?
   b. How many unique ideas did the groups have?
   c. How do you feel after you think of a new, creative idea?
   d. How important is creativity in entrepreneurship?
   e. How can we bring more creativity into our lives on a regular basis?

Category 6

Business Exercises

Use these exercises to explore business issues and strategies. Each member reflects on the specific topic first, then presents back to the Forum.

Refer to Part 1 of this book, Planning Your Retreat, for information on how to facilitate exercises. Time estimates for individual exercises are based on an 8-person Forum. Adjust the time estimates as needed to accommodate the size of your Forum.

Category 6 Exercises

forumsherpa

One Page Business Plan

The One Page Business Plan is an opportunity for Forum members to think strategically about their business. This exercise was a precursor to many popular versions of the strategic one-page plan.

Objectives

- To think at a high, strategic level about your business
- To learn more about each other's businesses

Facilitator Info

Depth Level:	Light
Facilitation Skills:	Basic
Estimated Time:	2 hours
Tools Needed:	Pens/pencils
Handouts:	One Page Business Plan Worksheet
Pre-work:	None
Notes:	• The One Page Business Plan is a great exercise to help you step back from the daily operations and refocus on your company at a 50,000 foot level. • There are several forms of the 1 page business plan, offered in books and seminars. • Sharing the plan is an excellent means of communicating your vision to your company, your peers and your family. • Review the plan at least once a year and make adjustments as needed.
Author/Source:	"CEO Tools", adapted for Forum

Facilitator Instructions

1) Explain the objective of the exercise. Distribute copies of the One Page Business Plan worksheet.
2) Discuss the components of the One Page Business Plan (see notes on next page).
3) Ask people to work independently for 30 minutes to write their one page Business Plan.
4) Bring everyone back together. One at a time, ask each person to share their one page Business Plan.
5) Allow time for questions at the end of each plan. Allot 10 minutes per person for presentation of the plan and Q&A.
6) Debrief on the exercise

One Page Business Plan, continued

Worksheet Components

\<your company name/logo\> **One Page Business Plan**
Goal/Mission
Unique Differentiator
Customer and Purpose
Strategy
Statistics

Explain the sections of the One Page Business Plan as described below.

- The Goal/Mission section states your primary, overall goal and/or purpose. It can include one or two key company-wide performance objectives. Think long term, minimum 3 years.
- The Unique Differentiator is a short description (25 words or less) of your niche, the thing you do differently and/or better than anyone else. It describes what you sell from the customer's viewpoint.
- The Customer and Purpose identifies your target customer and the purpose describes how you serve them.
- The Strategy explains where the company needs to go and how everyone will help get it there. Focus on long term strategy here (one to three years), not short term tactical plans.
- Include relevant Statistics about the company, for example: number of customers, number of employees, revenues, profit margins, length of sales cycle, etc.

One Page Business Plan Worksheet

Company Name: _____

Goal/Mission

Unique Differentiator

Customer and Purpose

Strategy

Statistics

Business Bio

The Business Bio exercise is a fast, efficient way for Forum members to share basic information about their businesses. It can be used by new and old Forums. It can also be helpful when a new member joins an existing Forum.

Objectives

- To compile a Business Bio about your company
- To learn basic information about each other's businesses

Facilitator Info

Depth Level:	Light
Facilitation Skills:	Basic
Estimated Time:	90 minutes
Tools Needed:	Pens/pencils
Handouts:	Business Bio Worksheet
Pre-work:	None
Notes:	• This is an excellent exercise for new Forums who don't yet know the basics about each other's businesses. • Members with multiple companies should either select their primary company, or complete multiple copies of the Business Bio.
Author/Source:	Ellie Byrd

Facilitator Instructions

1) Explain the objective of the exercise.
2) Distribute copies of the Business Bio worksheet.
3) Ask each member to work independently to complete the worksheet. Allow 20 minutes for this.
4) Bring the Forum members back together to present their Business Bio. Allow 10 minutes per person, including questions and answers.
5) As a Forum, identify other business topics that the group would like to discuss in future meetings. Keep a list of these topics for future reference.

Business Bio Worksheet

Legal	
Company Name:	
Legal Form of Business:	
Headquarters Location:	
Additional Locations:	
Year Founded and By Whom:	
Ownership: (list names and percentages)	

Business Description	
Type of Business: (industry or brief description)	
Target Customer:	
Products Offered:(list major product lines)	
Services Offered:(list major service lines)	
Sales Strategy:(one sentence)	
Unique Differentiator:	

Business Stats	
Top 3 Customers:	1) 2) 3)
Current # of Employees:	
Current # of Customers:	
Marketing Program: (list top 3 marketing initiatives)	1) 2) 3)
Annual Revenues (last year):	$
Target Revenues (this year):	$
Percentage likelihood of achieving target revenues:	% -
Key Competitors:	1) 2) 3)

Financial Disclosure

In the Financial Disclosure exercise, each person shares specific information about the financial condition of their company. Knowing this information about our fellow Forum mates helps us understand each other's financial position and perspectives better.

Objectives

- To learn more about each other's businesses
- To share financial data

Facilitator Info

Depth Level:	Medium
Facilitation Skills:	Medium
Estimated Time:	2 hours, 10 minutes
Tools Needed:	None
Handouts:	None
Pre-work:	Financial Disclosure Worksheet
Notes:	Members may feel somewhat vulnerable in this exercise.
Author/Source:	Ellie Byrd

Facilitator Instructions

1) Before the retreat, distribute the Financial Disclosure worksheet. Ask everyone to complete the worksheet and bring it to the retreat along with copies for everyone. (Be sure to allow ample time – it may take more time than you expect for people to gather this information.)
2) Note that all copies of the worksheets will be shredded after the exercise is complete.
3) Remind everyone that it's important not to be critical or judgmental of someone's financial position.
4) Remind everyone of the private nature of this exercise and the importance of confidentiality.
5) Give each person 10 minutes to present their financial information, and allow 5 minutes for questions and answers at the end. (Total 15 minutes per person.)

Debrief Questions

a) After everyone has shared their information, engage in the following debrief questions:
   i. How did it feel to disclose this level of financial information to your Forum?
   ii. What did you learn about each other during this exercise?
   iii. Are you going to make any changes in how you handle your finances as a result of this exercise?
b) Shred the worksheets!

Financial Disclosure Worksheet

Complete the Balance Sheet and Profit & Loss Statement information as requested below.
As of date: _____

Balance Sheet		
Cash in Bank:	$	
Current Assets:	$	
Fixed Assets:	$	
Other Assets:	$	
Current Liabilities:	$	
Long Term Liabilities:	$	
Stockholder/Owner Equity	$	

P&L	2 Years ago	Last Year	This Year (to-date)
Revenues	$	$	$
Cost of Goods Sold	$	$	$
G & A Expenses	$	$	$
Net Profit	$	$	$

Answer the following questions.
1) How often do you personally review your company financial statements?
2) How often do you meet with your CPA each year?
3) Describe the pricing of your products and/or services.
4) What are your company's top five line item costs or expenses on an annual basis?
   a) Line item: _____   Amount $_____
   b) Line item: _____   Amount $_____
   c) Line item: _____   Amount $_____
   d) Line item: _____   Amount $_____
   e) Line item: _____   Amount $_____
5) Identify three Key Performance Indicators (KPIs) for your business. These are numbers that you review (or that you should review) on a regular basis to assess your company's health and progress. Describe why these three indicators are so important to your business.
   a) Key Performance Indicator #1:
      i) Describe it.
      ii) Why is it important to your business?
      iii) What number indicates that things are good?
      iv) What number indicates a red flag?
   b) Key Performance Indicator #2:
      i) Describe it.
      ii) Why is it important to your business?
      iii) What number indicates that things are good?
      iv) What number indicates a red flag?
   c) Key Performance Indicator #3:
      i) Describe it.
      ii) Why is it important to your business?
      iii) What number indicates that things are good?
      iv) What number indicates a red flag?

Job Satisfaction Profile

The Job Satisfaction Profile asks members to contemplate how satisfied they are in their current work role. Seventeen different aspects of work are rated on a scale of 1 to 5. Some of these aspects can be easily changed, others cannot. Different aspects are more important to some people than to others.

Objectives

- To help clarify what we enjoy about our work
- To identify our level of satisfaction with our business/professional situation at this moment in time
- To contemplate possible changes in various aspects of our work life
- To learn about each other's daily work life

Facilitator Info

Depth Level:	Light
Facilitation Skills:	Basic
Estimated Time:	1 hour
Tools Needed:	Pens/pencils
Handouts:	Copies of Job Satisfaction Profile Form
Pre-work:	None
Notes:	None
Author/Source:	"Team Games for Trainers", adapted for Forum

Facilitator Instructions

1) Explain the objectives of the exercise.
2) Distribute copies of the Job Satisfaction Profile Form and ask Forum members to complete it. Allow 10 minutes for this. Write the five questions below on the flip chart while they're completing the worksheet.
3) Ask each Forum member to present their results, focusing on the following five questions. Allow 5 minutes per person.
   a. What are your totals in each of the five columns?
   b. What do you like best and least about your work?
   c. Where could you make changes that would improve your job satisfaction?
   d. If you could be doing something completely different, what comes to mind first?
   e. Overall, how would you rate your current job satisfaction?

Job Satisfaction Profile Form

Place an X on the rating scale after each item to indicate your level of satisfaction. Use this chart for your ratings:

1 = completely dissatisfied,
2 = somewhat dissatisfied
3 = neither satisfied or dissatisfied
4 = somewhat satisfied
5 = completely satisfied

#		1	2	3	4	5
1	the industry I am in					
2	the nature of the work I do every day					
3	the people I work with					
4	my compensation package					
5	my commute to the office					
6	my work environment – parking, building, on-site amenities, comfort					
7	my office – size, comfort, efficiency, location, view					
8	my work schedule (hours worked, start and end time)					
9	my work-related stress level					
10	technical support systems					
11	administrative and staff support					
12	support from my management team					
13	pure enjoyment of what I do					
14	my sense of accomplishment					
15	my sense of pride in what I do					
16	my opportunity to learn and grow					
17	the value I feel my work provides to society					
	Totals per column:					

What I like best about my work is:

_____

What I like least about my work is:

_____

Three Challenges

In the Three Challenges exercise, members think about three serious issues that are challenging them and/or their business. After contemplating possible solutions and next steps, the Forum provides additional feedback and support.

Objectives

- Identify challenges facing you in your business
- Share areas of concern and weaknesses
- Learn more about each other
- Identify possible ways to help each other overcome the challenges

Facilitator Info

Depth Level:	Medium
Facilitation Skills:	Medium
Estimated Time:	90 minutes
Tools Needed:	Flipchart, markers
Handouts:	Three Challenges Worksheet
Pre-work:	None
Notes:	<ul><li>This worksheet is better to complete on retreat, after having been away from the office for one or two days.</li><li>Keep a parking lot of potential Forum presentation topics that may come out of these issues.</li></ul>
Author/Source:	Ellie Byrd

Facilitator Instructions

1) Explain the objectives of the exercise and walk through the process.
2) Distribute the Three Challenges Worksheet.
3) Give participants 20 minutes to think through their challenges and complete the worksheet.
4) Have each member present their worksheet, talking about the challenges they are facing and their ideas for resolving it. There should be no interruptions while the member is presenting.
5) After each member presents, allow other members to offer relevant experience, or brainstorm on ideas that may be helpful.
6) Encourage members to keep notes of commitments they make to other members to help them with their challenges, for example: email a sample stock option plan, connect the member with a commercial realtor friend, etc.

Three Challenges Worksheet

Think about the three most critical issues facing you in your business today. Write down these issues in order of importance. Then complete the remainder of the table below.

Challenge	What are you doing about it or what do you plant to do about it?	What help do you need to face it or resolve it?
1.		
2.		
3.		

Notes

_____
_____
_____
_____
_____
_____
_____
_____
_____
_____
_____
_____
_____

Commitments to help other Forum Members

_____
_____
_____
_____
_____

Career Lifeline

The Career Lifeline exercise is an opportunity to reflect back on all the jobs you've ever had and what you learned at each one. Sharing this information with the Forum helps people understand each other's perspectives better. This exercise can be self-revealing.

Objectives

- To share business backgrounds with each other
- To learn more about fellow Forum members
- To identify patterns in work history

Facilitator Info

Depth Level:	Medium
Facilitation Skills:	Basic
Estimated Time:	2 hours
Tools Needed:	Flipchart, markers
Handouts:	Participants' Career Lifeline Worksheet
Pre-work:	None
Notes:	• Be sure to use a pencil to fill this out – there is usually lots of erasing! • Optionally, the worksheet can be completed in advance.
Author/Source:	Ellie Byrd

Facilitator Instructions

1) Explain the objectives of the exercise and walk through the process.
2) Provide each person with a Career Lifeline Worksheet.
3) Give participant's 20 minutes to complete their worksheet. While members are completing their worksheets, write three questions on the flipchart.
4) Have each member present their worksheet, talking through their work history. Allow 10 minutes per person.
5) Ask each member to answer the three questions on the flipchart.

Flipchart Questions – Self Analysis

> 1. Of all the jobs and positions you have held, which one was most rewarding? Why?
>
> 2. Which position was the most challenging? Why?
>
> 3. From whom did you learn the most in your business career? What did you learn?

6) Ask participants if they experienced any "aha's" during this exercise.

Career Lifeline Worksheet

Complete the chart below for EVERY job you have ever held in your life. (Yes, include mowing yards, delivering papers and flipping hamburgers at McDonald's!) You can be approximate on the details.

Put the list in chronological order. Use the back of the paper if necessary.

Your age	Job/position description	How much $$ were you paid?	Were you happy?	What did you learn while working there?

Sales Call

The Sales Call exercise is a great opportunity for members to tweak their sales pitch and get candid feedback from highly educated, non-customers. Preparation is critical to a successful exercise. Members learn interesting facts about each other and their businesses.

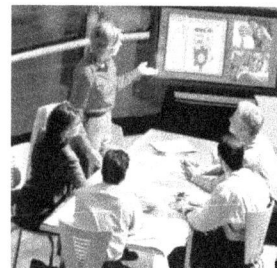

Objectives

- To learn more about each other's businesses
- To observe our own comfort level at selling our own products and services
- To get feedback on our sales pitch

Facilitator Info

Depth Level:	Medium
Facilitation Skills:	Basic
Estimated Time:	3 hours, 30 minutes
Tools Needed:	Props, products, flipchart, markers, projector and screen (if needed to demonstrate your product)
Handouts:	None
Pre-work:	Each person prepares a sales presentation, as if the Forum is a room full of potential customers.
Notes:	<ul><li>This exercise can be a lot of fun as well as informative.</li><li>As a variation, have each person present their business as if they were trying to convince a high-level, key employee to come and work for them.</li></ul>
Author/Source:	Ellie Byrd

Facilitator Instructions

1) Everyone needs to prepare for this in advance, as if they were giving a sales presentation to a room full of potential clients. Encourage people to bring props, handouts, sample products, etc.
2) Give each person 20 minutes to make their sales pitch.
   a. When presenting your sales pitch, you can use props, products, marketing materials and presentation materials (e.g., PowerPoint).
   b. The Forum should act like a room full of potential clients, asking questions as if they were a buyer.
3) After a person finishes their pitch, allow 5 minutes for comments, Q&A and experience sharing. Remind people that this should be done in a non-judgmental, non-critical manner.

Headlines!

In the Headlines! exercise, Forum members are asked to contemplate potential risks that could befall their business. As a result, people learn more about each other's businesses while increasing awareness of the risks to their own business.

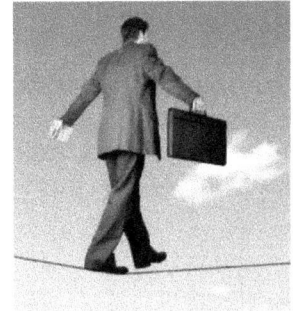

Objectives

- To consider areas where members' businesses may be at risk
- To learn more about each other's businesses

Facilitator Info

Depth Level:	Medium
Facilitation Skills:	Basic
Estimated Time:	60 minutes
Tools Needed:	Paper, pens/pencils
Handouts:	None
Pre-work:	None
Notes:	A variation of this exercise has each member develop an action plan on how they will work to better protect and prepare their business for potential disasters. This could be reported on periodically at Forum meetings. The Forum can be an excellent source of accountability if invited to provide it.
Author/Source:	Terry Plochman

Facilitator Instructions

1) Introduce the exercise as follows: "We are all one headline away from bankruptcy. Think about the type of catastrophes that could put you into bankruptcy."
2) Ask members to write down 2 to 3 headlines that would put them out of business and that could actually happen. Give people about 15 minutes to do this. Think about natural disasters, government regulations, legal issues, market shifts, etc.
3) Write down the following questions on the flipchart.
    a. What steps could you take to avoid this disaster?
    b. How would your family be affected if you lost your business?
    c. How would you be affected if you lost your business?
    d. How attached is your personal identity to your business?
4) Ask each person to share their headlines and answer the questions on the flipchart. Allow about 5 minutes per person.

Exit Strategy

The Exit Strategy exercise is an opportunity for the Forum to have a candid conversation about how people plan to exit their business. Members learn about previous exits through experience sharing, then contemplate how they might exit their own business. This exercise helps members learn more about each other's business and their desired end game, while considering their own exit.

Objectives

- To think about your exit strategy for your business
- To learn from each other's experiences
- To discuss your hopes for the future

Facilitator Info

Depth Level:	Medium
Facilitation Skills:	Medium
Estimated Time:	90 minutes
Tools Needed:	Flipchart, markers
Handouts:	None
Pre-work:	None
Notes:	Some Forums like to bring in an expert to talk with them about exit strategies, valuations, post-sale problems, etc. before or after this exercise. This exercise tends to be more powerful when it is done on the second or third day of the retreat, after being away from the minutiae of working "in the business" for a while.
Author/Source:	Ellie Byrd

Facilitator Instructions

1) Explain the objectives of the exercise.
2) Write the discussion questions on the flipchart before the exercise begins.

Selling Questions

First, have anyone who has sold a business, closed a business or gone out of business share their experience. Allow up to 5 minutes per experience.

- How long ago did this take place?
- What were the circumstances surrounding the exit?
- Were you pleased with the outcome?
- What did you learn from the experience?

Exit Strategy, continued

End Game Questions

Next, have each person answer the following questions:

- How long do you plan to stay in your current business?
- What is your ideal exit strategy?
- If you were to sell your company today, how much do you think it would be worth?
- What is your magic number? In other words, if someone walked up to you today and offered you a specific amount of money for your business that you would happily accept, what would the number be?
- What could you be doing right now to increase the value of your company over the next three years? Try to think of three things.
- How are businesses in your industry typically valued – book value, revenues multiplier, profit multiplier, inventory, intellectual property, etc.?

What's Next?

Finally, have each person think ahead. Assume they have just sold their business and answer these questions:

- You have just sold your business and the transaction is final. Aside from an employment agreement, what would you like to do next? Name three possibilities.
- Will you take a break from work for a while? If so, name three things you would like to do on a break.
- As a group, decide if there are other issues related to this topic that the Forum would like to explore in future meetings.

Category 7
Personal Exercises

Use these exercises for introspective thinking. Each member analyzes themselves first, then shares their thoughts and self-discoveries with the Forum. Members learn about themselves, learn from each other and learn more about each other.

Refer to Part 1 of this book, Planning Your Retreat, for information on how to facilitate exercises. Time estimates for individual exercises are based on an 8-person Forum. Adjust the time estimates as needed to accommodate the size of your Forum.

Category 7 Exercises

Creating a Personal Vision: Dialogue with a Wisdom Figure

Creating a Personal Vision: Dialogue with a Wisdom Figure is an introspective, thought-provoking exercise that taps into each person's inner wisdom. Through a combination of visualization and thoughtful contemplation, each person develops a vision for their own future.

Objectives

- To create a personal vision for the future
- To learn more about fellow Forum members' hopes and dreams

Facilitator Info

Depth Level:	High
Facilitation Skills:	Medium
Estimated Time:	2 hours
Tools Needed:	Pens/pencils, flipchart, markers
Handouts:	Copies of Key Life Questions and Wisdom Figure Dialogue Questions
Pre-work:	None
Notes:	• This exercise is a good predecessor to a Team Visioning exercise. Forums whose members are excited about their individual futures are more vital and resourceful than members who feel stuck or are unclear in their life purposes. • Although the questions could be distributed and answered as pre-work, part of the impact of this exercise involves thinking through these issues when you are in a quiet, peaceful retreat setting.
Author/Source:	"Building Team Spirit", adapted for Forum

Facilitator Instructions

1) Suggest that everyone releases the tensions of the day, relax, breathe deeply and listen to their inner voices. From this place of quiet, ask people to reflect on all of the people in their lives who have served as a source of wisdom and inspiration to them. Write their names on the notepad. The quantity is not important. From their list, ask them to select the one person who has served as their greatest source of wisdom. Allow 5 minutes for this.

2) Ask each person to turn to the person sitting closest to them and share the name of the person they chose and why they chose this person. Allow 5 minutes for this exchange.

3) Next, explain that everyone will be working independently on the next part of the exercise. Emphasize that vocation is an inner knowing or calling forth of our energies and resources to serve others. The secret is in listening to that inner knowing.

4) Distribute the Key Life Questions, which is a series of life-probing questions. Allow 20 minutes for everyone to complete these questions.

5) After everyone has completed the Key Life Questions, you are ready to move on to the next section. Explain that before they can have meaningfully dialogues with their wisdom figures, you would like to pose a question to them – "Are you willing to have a breakthrough in your life? Such a breakthrough will require that you take full responsibility for shifting your obstacles into opportunities. Are you willing to do that?"

Creating a Personal Vision, continued

Facilitator Instructions, continued

6) Ask people to enter into an imaginary dialogue with their wisdom figure through a series of questions. Distribute the Wisdom Figure Dialogue Questions handout.
7) As you read each question, first write down what you think your wisdom figure would say to you. Then, write down any responses and observations you may have yourself. Allow 35 minutes for everyone to complete these questions. Don't rush. Give yourself the gift of introspective thought.

Discussion Questions

After everyone has completed the questions, give each person the opportunity to share their reflections. Write these questions on a flipchart to start the conversation flowing for each person.

    a.   What did you observe as you completed the various phases of the exercise?
    b.   What did you notice about yourself?
    c.   How are you feeling about your future?
    d.   How do you feel about the obstacles you are facing?

Key Life Questions

1) What is the greatest source of passion in your life?

_____
_____
_____
_____
_____

2) What is it that you do that gives you the most pleasure?

_____
_____
_____
_____
_____

3) What do you most enjoy doing avocationally? Vocationally?

_____
_____
_____
_____
_____

4) What are the major transitions that you have made or contemplated making in your life?

_____
_____
_____
_____
_____

5) If you could do anything that you wished in the world, what would that one thing be?

_____
_____
_____
_____
_____

6) Where would you like to be in five years?

_____
_____
_____
_____
_____

7) What are the obstacles in the way of your achieving your five year vision?

_____
_____
_____
_____
_____

Wisdom Figure Dialogue Questions

Respond to each of the following questions, taking approximately three to five minutes per question, providing feedback from your wisdom figure, then observations and reactions for yourself.

1) What resources do you perceive I have that can help me to realize the future that I want to create for myself?
Wisdom Figure input: _____
_____
_____

My thoughts: _____
_____
_____

2) What coaching do you have for me, given your knowledge of me and sensitivity to my strengths and counterproductive traits?
Wisdom Figure input: _____
_____
_____

My thoughts: _____
_____
_____

3) Do you believe that what I am doing now is helpful for building the kind of future I want?
Wisdom Figure input: _____
_____
_____

My thoughts: _____
_____
_____

4) How can my Forum help me to achieve the future I am creating?
Wisdom Figure input: _____
_____
_____

My thoughts: _____
_____
_____

5) Who do you believe I should consult about the future that I want to create?
Wisdom Figure input: _____
_____
_____

My thoughts: _____
_____
_____

Creating a Personal Vision, continued

6) What do you perceive to be my greatest inner strength that I can draw upon to move to the future that I want?

Wisdom Figure input: _____
_____
_____

My thoughts: _____
_____
_____

7) What should I do right now to accomplish the future I want? And then what?... And then what?.... And then what.... And then what?

Wisdom Figure input: _____
_____
_____

My thoughts: _____
_____
_____

Personal Financial Disclosure

The Personal Financial Disclosure exercise is an opportunity for Forum members to discuss a complex and sensitive issue – money! Through a series of increasingly revealing questions, people share their current financial condition, their views about money and their financial plan for the future. People sometimes learn that they have misconceptions about each other's financial position. Forums often feel an increased bonding after this exercise.

Objectives

- To bring a new level of understanding among Forum members on personal finances
- To learn from each other and get ideas on how to handle personal finances
- To gain a new perspective and awareness of money management

Facilitator Info

Depth Level:	High
Facilitation Skills:	Advanced
Estimated Time:	4 hours
Tools Needed:	None
Handouts:	Personal Financial Disclosure Worksheet
Pre-work:	Complete the worksheet in advance.
Notes:	• This exercise could be divided into sections, allowing approximately one hour for each of the four main sections. • This exercise could be done at regular Forum meetings over a period of several months. Use one of the four Discussions at each meeting. • The four Discussions increase in level of disclosure, so keep them in order.
Author/Source:	Ellie Byrd

Facilitator Instructions

1) Distribute Personal Financial Disclosure worksheet before the retreat. Ask everyone to complete the worksheet in advance.
2) At the retreat, discuss each section individually. For example, start with Discussion 1 and have each member share their answers to the questions in Discussion 1 until everyone has shared. Then move to Discussion 2 and have everyone share their information for that section only. Then move to Discussion 3, and so on.
3) It is fine for members to ask questions when someone is sharing their information, but remind everyone not to be judgmental or critical.
4) Remind everyone of the private nature of this exercise and the importance of confidentiality.

Personal Financial Disclosure Worksheet

Discussion 1: Your Personal Views on Money and Finances

Answer the following questions.

1) How would you describe managing finances? For example, do you find it irritating, fun, interesting, a chore, etc.

2) Describe your family's financial condition when you were a child. Were you rich, middle class, poor? How did this affect you?

3) Did your parents teach you money management skills when you were young?

4) Do you have a personal or household budget?

5) How often do you review your finances to see if you are living within your means?

6) Do you enjoy shopping?

7) Do you spend more money than you earn?

8) Do you have credit card debt that you are paying off over time?

9) Do you think it's better to pay by cash or credit? Why?

10) If you are married, how are your finances handled? Is everything shared, separate, or somewhere in the middle?

11) If you are married, do finances cause problems in your relationship? If so, how?

12) If you have children, what are you teaching them about money? How?

Personal Financial Disclosure Worksheet, continued

Discussion 2: How you spend your money

Think of the ten biggest items you spend money on each year. These can be categories, such as mortgage, car payment, utilities, clothes, kid's school, travel, eating out, insurance, etc. List the items in order, with the biggest item first.

	Expense Item/Category	Monthly	Annually
1		$	$
2		$	$
3		$	$
4		$	$
5		$	$
6		$	$
7		$	$
8		$	$
9		$	$
10		$	$

1) Are you pleased with these 10 items/categories? If not, where would you like to make changes?

2) Do you regularly put money aside for savings? How much?

3) Do you invest in a tax-deferred retirement plan? How much?

4) How are your investments allocated?

5) Do you have life insurance?

6) Do you meet with a financial planner to help you with your investments?

7) Share a couple of your favorite tips and tricks that enable you to save money on expenses.

Personal Financial Disclosure Worksheet, continued

Discussion 3: Your Earning Power

List all your sources of income. You may have only one source of income, or you may have several categories such as: real estate investments, sideline consulting, multiple businesses, etc. List the items in order, with the biggest item first.

	Income Item/Category	Monthly	Annually
1		$	$
2		$	$
3		$	$
4		$	$
5		$	$
6		$	$
7		$	$
8		$	$
9		$	$
10		$	$

1) Is your income enough to pay off debt and support your spending habits?

2) Are there other sources of income you would like to pursue? What are they?

3) How much money would you like to have when you retire? How old will you be then?

4) If you won $20 million dollars in the lottery tomorrow, what would you do with the money?

Personal Financial Disclosure Worksheet, continued

Discussion 4: Your Net Worth

Complete the following table by filling in the blanks. If something doesn't apply, leave it blank or write a zero in the box.

Assets	Current Value
Cash in the Bank	$
Securities, Stocks, Bonds, etc.	$
Retirement Savings	$
Other Investments	$
Primary Residence	$
Other Real Estate Holdings (re-sale value)	$
Automobiles, Boats, Planes, etc.	$
Debt Owed to you by others	$
Other Assets	$
Total Assets	$
Liabilities	**Current Value**
Credit card debt	$
Mortgage debt	$
Other loan debt	$
Other miscellaneous debt	$
Total Liabilities	$

Subtract your liabilities from your assets to determine your personal Net Worth: $_____

Discussion 5: Debrief

(To be completed at the retreat.)

Engage in an open discussion on the following questions:

1) How did it feel to disclose this level of financial information to your Forum?

2) What did you learn about each other during this exercise?

3) Are you going to make any changes in how you handle your finances as a result of this exercise?

Decisions

Decisions is an introspective exercise that helps people self-analyze their own decision-making process and learn from each other's experiences. By reviewing key decisions from the past, people learn techniques and strategies on how to make better decisions.

Objectives

- To reflect on the key decisions you have made in your life
- To reflect on your decision-making process
- To reflect on what you have learned from your decisions

Facilitator Info

Depth Level:	High
Facilitation Skills:	Medium
Estimated Time:	2 hours
Tools Needed:	None
Handouts:	Copies of the Decisions Worksheet
Pre-work:	Complete the Decisions Worksheet in advance.
Notes:	The "challenging decisions" that come out in step 2d under Facilitator Instructions can be a good source for future presentations.
Author/Source:	Bill Evans

Facilitator Instructions

1) Ask each person to complete the Decisions worksheet (below) before the retreat. Bring the completed worksheet with the answers to the retreat.
2) At the retreat, ask each person to answer the following questions. Allow approximately 10 minutes per person.
    a. Share one of your most difficult decisions, one of your best decisions and one of your worst decisions.
    b. What is your typical decision-making process?
        i. Do you ask others for input? Who do you ask?
        ii. Do you decide more with your heart or with your head?
        iii. How do you analyze your choices?
    c. Are you definitive about the decision, or do you tend to flip-flop?
    d. When you make decisions, are you a risk taker or are you more conservative?
    e. What is the most challenging decision you are facing right now?

Debrief Discussion

As a debrief, discuss the following questions as a group.

a) As a group, are there any patterns in our decisions – similar experiences, similar results?
b) What did you learn about each other from this exercise?
c) What did you learn about yourself from this exercise?

Decisions Worksheet

1) In your life, what is the **<u>most difficult decision</u>** you have made related to:
   a) Your business/work/career?
      i) What made it so difficult?
      ii) Explain.
   b) Your family?
      i) What made it so difficult?
      ii) Explain.
   c) You personally?
      i) What made it so difficult?
      ii) Explain
   d) To what extent were these decisions not only difficult, but also painful? If one of them was painful for you, rate it on a scale of 1 (low) to 10 (high).

2) In your life, what is the **<u>best decision</u>** you have made related to:
   a) Your business/work/career?
      i) Describe it.
      ii) What were/are the outcomes that resulted?
      iii) If anything, what did you learn?
   b) Your family?
      i) Describe it.
      ii) What were/are the outcomes that resulted?
      iii) If anything, what did you learn?
   c) You personally?
      i) Describe it.
      ii) What were/are the outcomes that resulted?
      iii) If anything, what did you learn?

3) In your life, what is the **<u>worst decision</u>** you have made related to:
   a) Your business/work/career?
      i) What happened?
      ii) Any lessons learned?
   b) Your family?
      i) What happened?
      ii) Any lessons learned?
   c) You personally?
      i) What happened?
      ii) Any lessons learned?

4) What major decisions are you most **<u>looking forward</u>** to making in the future?
   a) Business/work/career.
   b) Family
   c) Personally

5) What decisions are you most **<u>dreading</u>** to make in the future that you know you will face?
   a) Business/work/career
   b) Family
   c) Personally

6) What do you believe your life will be like in the future, 25 years from today?
   a) Business/work/career
   b) Family
   c) Personally

Freedom from the Rock I Am Carrying

Freedom from the Rock I Am Carrying is an exercise that invites members to contemplate a burden or a challenge they are dealing with. Members use the symbolism of a physical rock to consider the potential of reducing or eliminating the issue. People often feel a sense of calm regarding the specific burden they chose to deal with.

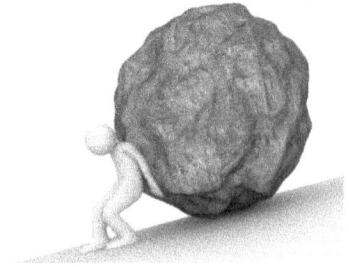

Objectives
- To raise awareness of the stresses and burdens we carry that keep us from feeling freer and lighter in life
- To work on developing a strategy to diminish or free us from burdens

Facilitator Info

Depth Level:	High
Facilitation Skills:	Medium
Estimated Time:	1 hour
Tools Needed:	An assortment of paint jars, paint brushes and rocks
Handouts:	None
Pre-work:	None
Notes:	This exercise should take place outdoors if possible.
Author/Source:	Jorge Cherbosque

Facilitator Instructions
1) Ask members to think of a burden they are carrying, such as guilt, an over-commitment to something they don't really want to do, etc.
2) Have each member pick up a rock to symbolize the burden they are carrying. Place the rock in their shoe and walk with it for about 3 minutes.
3) Invite members to paint or write anything on their rock and share it with the group.
4) At the end of the retreat, take the members to a place where they can throw their rock, replace it with a smaller one, or keep it as a reminder.

Debrief Questions
As a group, debrief with the following questions:
   a) How did it feel to carry your rock?
   b) How did it feel to let it go, exchange it or keep it?
   c) What would it take for you to be free from this rock?

Life Assessment Survey

The Life Assessment Survey is an independent, self-administered
view of life. Each person contemplates a variety of life factors
by rating themselves in 20 different areas.

Objectives

- To self-analyze how well Forum members think they are doing in various aspects of their life
- To consider changes that each person could make to improve their quality of life

Facilitator Info

Depth Level:	Medium
Facilitation Skills:	Medium
Estimated Time:	1½ hours
Tools Needed:	Pens/pencils
Handouts:	Life Assessment Survey Form
Pre-work:	None
Notes:	Don't let people criticize or challenge someone's rating. This is an exercise in self-discovery. Judgmental comments are not allowed, only support.
Author/Source:	Bill Evans

Facilitator Instructions

1) Explain the objective of the exercise as follows:

> "The Life Assessment Survey is designed to gather your perceptions of your life experience so far. It asks you to rate a number of significant variables that are linked to your overall level of life satisfaction and happiness.
>
> On each item, using a 1 to 10 scale (1 is low, 10 is high), rate how you see it right now. Perhaps 10 years ago you would have responded differently or maybe you will see it differently at some future time.
>
> Be as honest as you can be. You are doing this for you and no one else, including your Forum members. If you rate an item a "10", you won't have to defend it, nor will you have to defend an item rated "1". No one will be allowed to try to talk you out of a number. Each of you will be asked to share your responses.
>
> Some of you may be extremely analytical and find it hard to come up with a justification for your ratings. Just go with your gut feeling. No explanation or back-up information is required."

2) Distribute the Life Assessment Survey form and ask everyone to complete it. Allow about 15 minutes for this.
3) Ask each person to share their results, then answer the following questions.
   a. Are you pleased with the results?
   b. Were you surprised by anything?
   c. Would you like to make any changes as a result of this assessment?

Life Assessment Survey Form

Date: _____   Name: _____

On each of the following items, enter the number that you believe is true for you at this point in your life. If the question doesn't apply to you skip it.

What is your perception of how you have done in terms of...   (1 = low, 10 = high)

1) Finding meaningful and fulfilling work?   _____

2) Finding a suitable spouse/partner?   _____

3) Building a successful relationship with your spouse/partner?   _____

4) Rearing your children?   _____

5) Building and/or maintaining a close relationship with your parents?   _____

6) Building and/or maintaining a close relationship with your siblings?   _____

7) Developing close friendships?   _____

8) Stewarding your financial resources?   _____

9) Living up to your intellectual potential (are you still curious)?   _____

10) Nurturing your spiritual potential?   _____

11) Dealing with your fears?   _____

12) Finding wisdom?   _____

13) Taking care of your physical health?   _____

14) Taking care of your emotional health?   _____

15) Being of service to others?   _____

16) Being at one with yourself?   _____

17) Accepting your limitations?   _____

18) Coming to terms with aging and your own mortality?   _____

19) Everyone at birth is "dealt a hand", so to speak. Rate the quality of the

     "hand" you were dealt.   _____

20) Overall, rate yourself on how well you believe you have played the game of

     life, given the hand you were dealt.   _____

Relationships in Conflict

Relationships in Conflict is an exercise that encourages Forum members to contemplate a relationship that needs improvement. Each person identifies a specific situation and answers a series of questions to move toward a possible solution.

Objectives

- To enable each member the opportunity to reflect on a personal relationship that is in conflict
- To consider options for how the conflict might be resolved
- To learn more about Forum members and offer support

Facilitator Info

Depth Level:	Medium
Facilitation Skills:	Medium
Estimated Time:	2 hours
Tools Needed:	Pens/pencils
Handouts:	Copies of the Relationships in Conflict Worksheet
Pre-work:	None
Notes:	None
Author/Source:	Bill Evans

Facilitator Instructions

1) Introduce the exercise and ask each person to think of someone in their life with whom they have an unresolved conflict... a conflict that they would like to resolve.
2) Distribute a copy of the Relationships in Conflict Worksheet and ask each person to answer the questions in writing.
3) Ask each person to share their responses (about 10 minutes per person).

Relationships in Conflict Worksheet

1) Who is the person? And what is your relationship to that person?

_____
_____
_____
_____

2) Describe the relationship as it is today.

_____
_____
_____
_____

3) Describe the relationship as you would like it to be.

_____
_____
_____
_____

4) Describe the conflict.

   a) What is the nature of the conflict?

_____
_____
_____
_____

   b) What would it take to resolve the conflict from your perspective?

_____
_____
_____
_____

   c) What do you believe it would take to resolve the conflict from the other person's perspective?

_____
_____
_____
_____

Values

The Values exercise helps Forum members contemplate their value system and what is most important to them. First the group compiles a list of values together, then each person is led through an exercise to discover their own most important values.

Objectives

- To reflect on the most important values in our lives
- To learn more about our fellow Forum members and what is important to them

Facilitator Info

Depth Level:	Medium
Facilitation Skills:	Medium
Estimated Time:	90 minutes
Tools Needed:	Flipchart, markers, large stack of 3x5 index cards (10 per person), pens/pencils
Handouts:	None
Pre-work:	None
Notes:	This exercise is especially relevant on a retreat dealing with life planning, life balance, etc.
Author/Source:	Terry Plochman

Facilitator Instructions

1) Hold a brainstorming session on the following question: "What are life's most important values?"
2) Capture all suggestions on a flipchart.
3) Once done, ask each person to write down the 10 items on the list that they value most. Write each item on a 3 x 5 index card, one item per card.
4) Ask each person to discard the three cards that are the least important to them.
5) Then, ask them to discard the next lowest three cards.
6) Then, ask them to discard the next lowest two cards, leaving only two more cards.
7) Ask them to write #1 and #2 on the two remaining cards according to rank.

Discussion Questions

Engage in a discussion where each person answers the following questions (approximately 5 minutes per person):

a. What were your top two values?
b. Why were they the highest? Describe what these two values mean to you.
c. What other words would you use to describe them?
d. How do you express that value in your life?
e. Do your checkbook, your calendar and other elements of your life reflect that value? If not, why?
f. How can you get your actions in line with your values?

Money and Values

Money and Values engages Forum members in a light-hearted exercise on a serious topic–our value system. After trading Values cards and play money to achieve their optimum value set, Forum members answer a series of questions regarding their choices.

Objectives

- To encourage interaction and self-disclosure about values
- To reveal Forum members' priorities for their values

Facilitator Info

Depth Level:	Light
Facilitation Skills:	Medium
Estimated Time:	1 hour
Tools Needed:	Three Values cards for each participant (3x5 cards, prepared in advance); $1000 in Monopoly money for each Forum member in several denominations
Handouts:	Reflections Questions
Pre-work:	None
Notes:	The Exchange Phase can get loud and chaotic.
Author/Source:	Unknown, adapted for Forum

Facilitator Instructions

Preparation
1) Create Value Cards (See the list of Value Card ideas on the next page.) You can hand write them on 3 x 5 cards or print them on card stock.

Setting the Stage
2) Explain the objectives of the exercise and walk through the process.
3) Give each participant three Values cards and $1,000 in play money.
4) Explain to the participants that they are about to participate in an exchange of Values cards. (If pressed about the objectives of the game, state that the goal is to possess the Values that matter most to them.)

Exchange Phase
5) Explain the ground rules for buying, selling and trading cards:
   a. Each person may buy, sell, or trade Value cards.
   b. Cards may be bought or sold for a mutually agreed upon price, or traded outright.
   c. You MUST sell or trade at least one of your Values cards sometime during the activity.
   d. You must end up with at least one Values card.
6) Ask if they have any questions.
7) Begin the exchange phase. Allow 10 minutes for this, then stop the process.
8) Handout the Reflection questions and give everyone about 10 minutes to fill them out.
9) Go around the room and ask each person to share their answers to the reflection questions. Limit each person to 1 or 2 minutes.

Money and Values, continued

Discussion Phase

    10) Write the following questions on the flipchart. (Do this in advance to save time.)

    11) Take one question at a time, and encourage a free form discussion of each question.

        a.   What did this experience tell you or reconfirm about your values?

        b.   What surprised you?

        c.   What did you learn about your fellow team members?

        d.   What values that are especially important to you were missing from the cards?

        e.   How can you apply what you have learned from this experience to your daily interactions with one another?

Value Cards – Ideas

Write a single value on each 3x5 card. Be sure you have enough cards so that each person will start with three values. Feel free to make up your own values.

1. To be successful
2. To be needed and to be important to others
3. To have good feelings about myself
4. To be a good conversationalist
5. To have my opinions respected
6. To develop my potential
7. To believe in myself
8. To be happy in all that I do
9. To be warm and sincere
10. To be a good parent
11. To make an impact on others
12. To have a stronger spiritual relationship
13. To be accepted
14. To live up to my convictions
15. To be at ease with other people
16. To never be lonely
17. To have self-confidence
18. To be financially secure
19. To be loved by a special few
20. To give of myself freely in helping others
21. To have a loving relationship with a significant other
22. To be an effective leader
23. To be very creative
24. To be considered different and unique
25. To be more open and vulnerable with others
26. To be less easily influenced
27. To be liked by everyone
28. To be free
29. To know myself better
30. To be more physically attractive

Money and Values, continued

Reflection Questions

Reflect on the exercise you have just completed by answering the following questions.

1) What were the original Values cards that you received?

2) Why did you keep them or trade them?

3) How much money did you have at the end of the experience?

4) Were you more interested in obtaining meaningful Values cards or in accumulating the most money possible?

5) Which Values card did you most wish to obtain?

6) Are you satisfied with the Values cards that you now have?

You will each share your answers to these questions. Then, the facilitator will lead you through a series of five discussion questions.

Achievements and Motivators

In the Achievements and Motivators exercise, Forum members reflect on their skills, talents and greatest achievements in life. The achievements become a catalyst to analyze what motivates us toward achievement. It is an introspective, thought-provoking exercise that helps Forum members learn more about themselves and each other.

Objectives

- To contemplate strengths, skills and talents along with our top ten greatest achievements.
- To identify the things that motivate us toward achievement
- To build understanding, respect and tolerance for each other and for different points of view

Facilitator Info

Depth Level:	Medium
Facilitation Skills:	Medium
Estimated Time:	2 hours
Tools Needed:	Flipchart, markers
Handouts:	Achievement Tree Worksheet, Motivators Chart
Pre-work:	None
Notes:	If time permits in step 5, you could ask each person to share their top 10 achievements. Allow an extra 3 minutes per person for this.
Author/Source:	"Team Games for Trainers – Fruits of Success", adapted for Forum

Facilitator Instructions

1) Distribute the Achievement Tree Worksheet.
2) Ask participants to complete the worksheet as explained below. Allow 15 minutes for this.
   a. Start at the roots of the tree and identify each root as a particular strength. Identify things such as talents, skills and knowledge. Label one strength per root and add more roots if needed.
   b. Label each fruit as a success – professional, personal or otherwise. Some examples include: a vacation house in the mountains, a good marriage, an award, weight loss, election to public office, etc. More examples are provided on the following page. Consider making copies of this for people to review for ideas, or simply read the achievements at the beginning of the exercise.
   c. Add the year that you achieved each success and add a number (1 to 10) to rank the importance of each achievement in order of priority.
3) Pair up with another person and present your trees to each other one at a time. Allow 5 minutes for this.

Achievements and Motivators, continued

Sample Achievements

Achievement is in the eye of the beholder. Something that may be easy for one person to achieve could be an overwhelming achievement for another person. Resist the temptation to compare yourself or compete with others. Focus on the achievements that were the most meaningful to you.

- Started my own company.
- Helped my high school football team to an 11–0 record my senior year.
- First person in my family to graduate from college.
- Became a millionaire by age 26.
- Reconciled with my father.
- Purchased my own house.
- Overcame poverty.
- Graduated magna cum laude.
- Got my pilot's license.
- Celebrated my 20 year anniversary – happily!
- Golfed an 89.
- Became an eagle scout.
- Paid my way thru college.
- Saved a life using CPR.
- Traveled to Europe after college.
- Immigrated to the United States.
- Learned to speak 4 languages fluently.
- Climbed Kilimanjaro.
- Had a featured article about me in the local business magazine.
- Read the Bible, cover to cover.
- Talked my sister off the ledge.
- Won an industry association award for excellence.
- Maintained a 3.85 GPA throughout college.
- Ran a marathon.
- Designed and built my own home at age 31.
- Took my Mom to Thailand.
- Was on Inc 500 list 3 years in a row.
- Forgave my mom at her funeral.
- Hit a home run my sophomore year.
- Stopped the cycle of abuse in my family.
- Was boxing champion at West Point.
- Made 10 people millionaires.
- Got my MBA.
- Have 3 great kids.
- Was All-State in football and baseball for three years.
- Got an A in organic chemistry.
- Helped my dad die.
- Served as Chamber Chapter President.

Achievements and Motivators, continued

Facilitator Instructions – Motivators Chart

1) Distribute the "Motivators Chart". Provide instructions for completing the chart:
   a. Copy the top ten achievements from the Achievements Tree Worksheet. Copy them in order by priority, 1 thru 10.
   b. For each achievement, go down the list of motivators and mark every motivator that contributed to the successful achievement of the goal.
   c. Total across the number of times a particular motivator has occurred and total down the number of motivators for each achievement.
2) After everyone has completed their Motivators Chart (about 10 minutes), ask each person to answer the four discussion questions below for the entire Forum. Allow 5 minutes per person.

Discussion Questions

Write these questions on the flipchart in advance, but cover up the questions until you reach this point in the exercise.

   a. Which three motivators are most prevalent for you?
   b. When did most of your achievements occur? Is there a time pattern (e.g. all were over 20 years ago, evenly spaced, etc.)?
   c. What is your #1 achievement, when did it occur and why is it so important to you?
   d. What surprised you most about this exercise, i.e. what did you learn about yourself?

Bonus Note

Facilitators who are knowledgeable in the field of motivation, e.g. internal/external and intrinsic/extrinsic motivators, may want to engage in further discussion on the following concepts.

Note the three groupings of motivators on the Motivators Chart.

- The first four motivators are external, extrinsic. These motivators are usually tied to ego and they may change and/or lack longevity based on life circumstances.

- The center four motivators (shaded) are internal, intrinsic. These motivators reflect our true, inner passion. Motivation is natural, simple and even easy.

- The bottom four motivators are internal extrinsic. While we're internally motivated by them, the motivation is generated by something or someone external.

Achievements Tree Worksheet

1) Start at the roots of the tree and identify each root as a particular strength. Identify such things as talents, skills and knowledge. Label one strength per root and add more roots if needed.

2) Label each fruit as an achievement or a success – professional, personal or otherwise. Some examples include: a vacation house in the mountains, a good marriage, an award, weight loss, election to public office, etc. It's okay to add more fruit if needed.

3) Add the year that you achieved each success and add a number (1 to 10) to the top 10 most important achievements in order of priority.

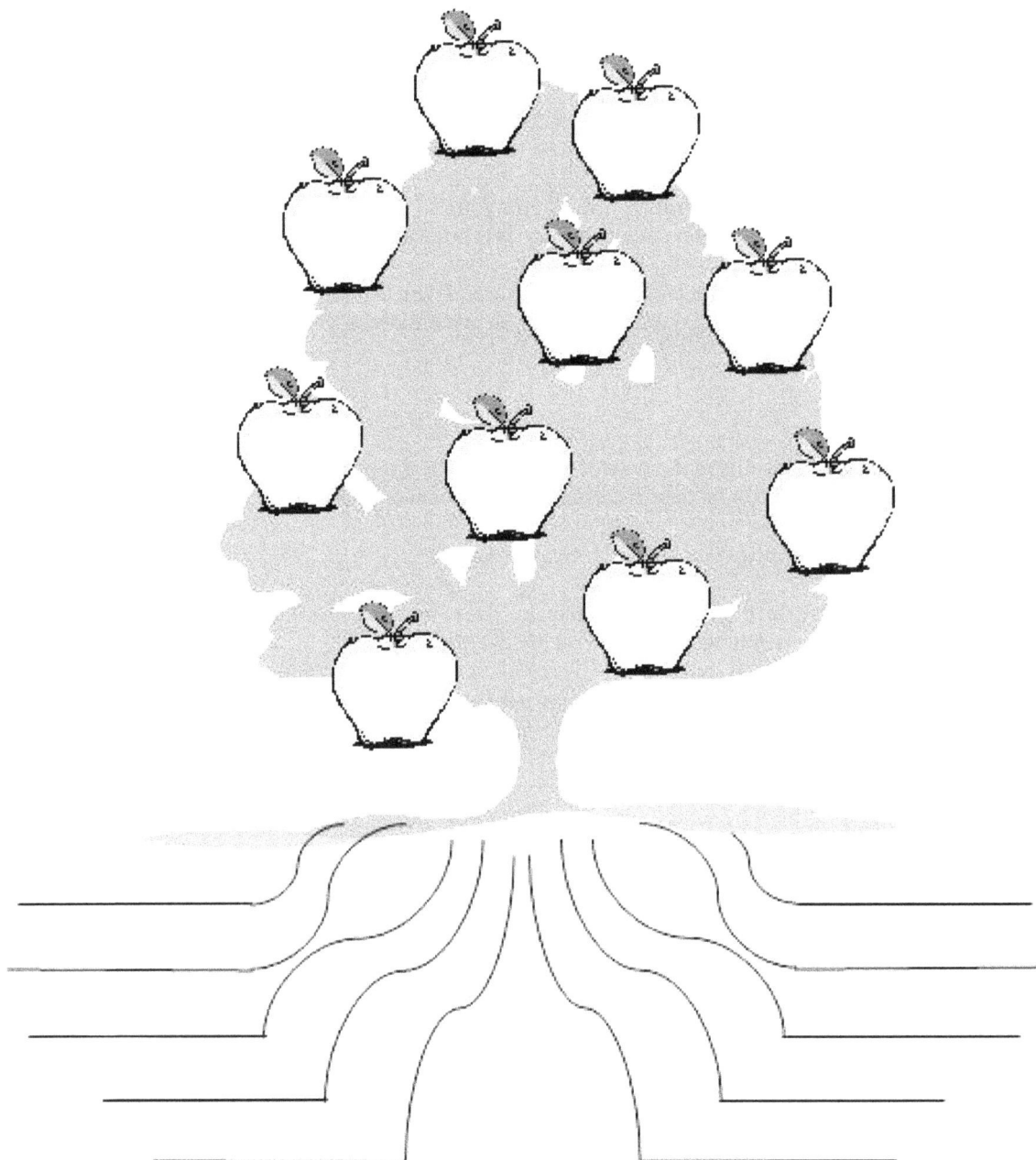

Motivators Chart

1) Copy the top ten achievements from the Achievement Tree Worksheet. Copy them in order by priority, 1 thru 10.
2) For each achievement, go down the list of motivators and mark every motivator that contributed to the successful achievement of the goal. You may have several motivators for each achievement.
3) Total across the number of times a particular motivator has occurred and total down the number of motivators for each achievement.

Priority:	1	2	3	4	5	6	7	8	9	10	Total
Achievements:											
Year:											
Motivators											
money or bonus											
competition											
recognition											
external pressure											
passion or pleasure											
sense of accomplishment											
security											
values or beliefs											
guilt											
winning											
friendship											
seeing the value it brings to others											
TOTAL											

Balance Wheels

The Balance Wheels exercise is a quick self-assessment on how balanced each person is in various aspects of life. Forum members rate their level of happiness on two wheels – one professional, one personal. Each wheel contains eight life aspects, such as enjoyment of work, financial compensation, family, spiritual, fun/free time, etc.

Objectives

- To analyze potential imbalances in members' lives
- To build understanding for each other and get to know each other better

Facilitator Info

Depth Level:	Medium
Facilitation Skills:	Medium
Estimated Time:	1 hour
Tools Needed:	Pens/pencils
Handouts:	Balance Wheels Worksheet
Pre-work:	None
Notes:	If time permits, you can add a question & answer period to the end of each person's presentation. Listen for possible presentation topics while people are presenting.
Author/Source:	Ellie Byrd

Facilitator Instructions

1) Explain the objective of the exercise.
2) Distribute the Balance Wheels worksheet and ask each member to self-rate their satisfaction in each area of the balance wheels. Connect the numbers to see how evenly the areas are balanced. Allow 10 minutes for this.
3) One at a time, ask each person to share their Balance Wheels with the Forum. Allow 5 minutes per person. Consider the following questions:
   a. How balanced are your wheels?
   b. Where are the most major imbalances?
   c. Is this an ongoing trend, or is something unique happening in your life right now?
   d. What could you do to achieve more balance in your life?
4) There should be no interruptions while a person is presenting. If time permits, questions and answers can be asked after each person shares.

Balance Wheels, continued

Balance Wheels Worksheet

On each balance wheel, circle the number that best describes your level of satisfaction in each area. 1 = very dissatisfied and 7 = very satisfied. Then draw lines to connect the dots. How balanced are your wheels? Imagine how well a bicycle would ride if the wheels were in this shape.

Professional Balance Wheel

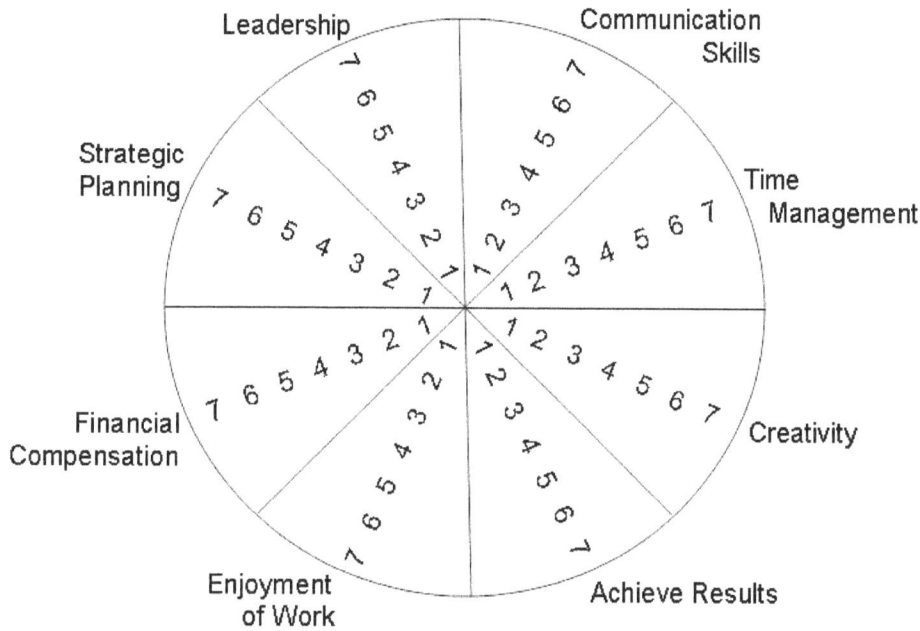

Personal Balance Wheel

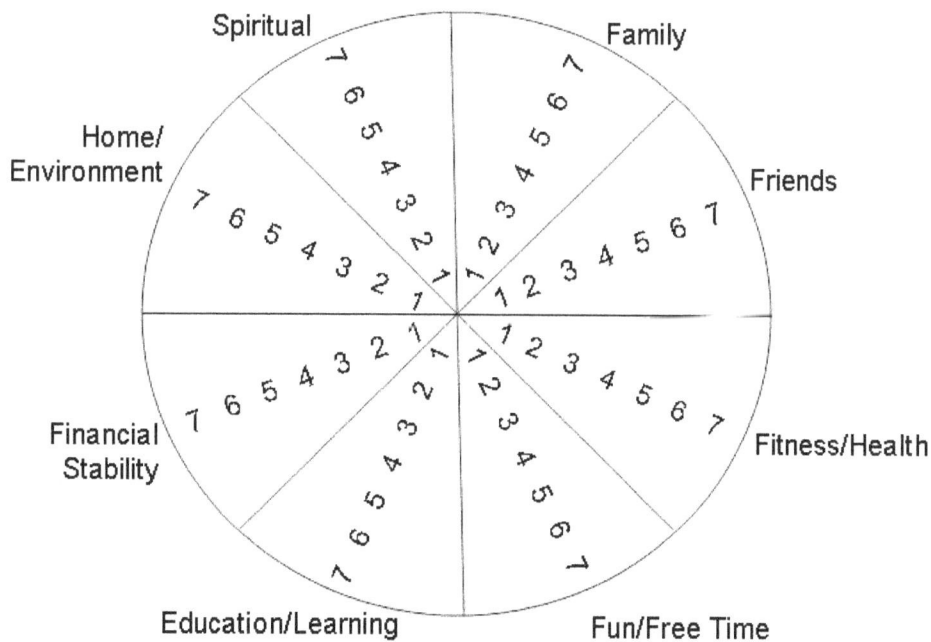

Life's Pie Chart

Life's Pie Chart is an exercise that will help participants have an increased awareness of balance in their lives. People develop an action plan to achieve better balance and overall happiness.

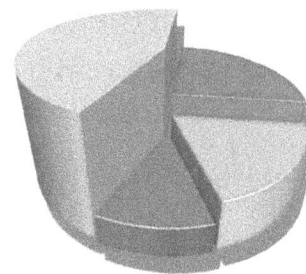

Objectives

- To help participants discover potential imbalances in their life
- To help participants identify strategies for achieving better life balance
- To build understanding for each other and get to know each other better
- To strengthen accountability among the group in supporting each other's life balance

Facilitator Info

Depth Level:	Medium
Facilitation Skills:	Medium
Estimated Time:	90 minutes
Tools Needed:	Pens/pencils
Handouts:	Life's Pie Chart Worksheet
Pre-work:	None
Notes:	One variation of this exercise is to develop a detailed action plan for each of the five areas on the "Life Pie Chart." If you do this, add 15 minutes for preparation time and three minutes per person for presenting.
Author/Source:	Ellie Byrd

Facilitator Instructions

1) Explain the objective of the exercise.
2) Distribute the Life's Pie Chart worksheet and explain how to fill it out.
   a. First, identify up to five areas of your life that consume most of your time. Note that sleep can be included as one of the areas, because a severe lack of sleep can have an impact on our lives.
   b. On a separate page, make a list of the type of activities that comprise each of the five areas.
   c. Next, on the Current Pie, draw a chart of how much time you spend in each of the five areas.
   d. On the Future Pie, draw a chart of how much time you would like to spend in each of the five areas.
   e. Think of three specific action items that will help you transition from the current pie to the future pie.
   f. Allow 15 minutes for people to complete the worksheet.
3) One at a time, ask each person to share their Life's Pie Chart. Allow 7 minutes per person. There should be no interruptions while a person is presenting.
   a. Discuss the five areas of importance.
   b. Talk about the most major discrepancies between the two pies. Why do these discrepancies exist?
   c. How difficult will it be to transition to the future pie?
4) If time permits, questions and answers can be asked after each person's presentation.

Life's Pie Chart Worksheet

1) Identify key aspects of your life (minimum 3, maximum 5).

Aspect 1) _____

Aspect 2) _____

Aspect 3) _____

Aspect 4) _____

Aspect 5) _____

2) On a separate sheet of paper, make a list of the activities you are including in each aspect.
3) Estimate your time for each aspect and draw your Pie Charts.

Pie Chart #1:

Current Chart
This is how I spend my time now.
Pie Segments:

_____% Aspect 1
_____% Aspect 2
_____% Aspect 3
_____% Aspect 4
_____% Aspect 5

Pie Chart #2

Future Chart
This is how I want to spend my time.
Pie Segments:

_____% Aspect 1
_____% Aspect 2
_____% Aspect 3
_____% Aspect 4
_____% Aspect 5

4) Identify three action items to move from your Current Pie Chart to your Future Pie Chart.

1. _____

2. _____

3. _____

High Hurdles

The High Hurdles exercise is an opportunity to gain focus and clarity on challenges while learning from the experiences of others. By reflecting on past challenges and lessons learned, and by discussing current issues and challenges, members often find opportunities to help and support each other.

Objectives

- To review major hurdles in life and identify trends
- To recognize current hurdles and identify strategies to overcome them
- To learn more about fellow Forum members
- To learn from each other's experiences

Facilitator Info

Depth Level:	High
Facilitation Skills:	Medium
Estimated Time:	3 hours
Tools Needed:	Pens/pencils
Handouts:	• Past High Hurdles Worksheet • Current High Hurdles Worksheet
Pre-work:	None
Notes:	• Hurdles can be business or personal in nature. • Optionally, you can have participants complete their worksheets in advance to save time. • One variation of this exercise is to specify the type of hurdle, such as business only, family only, personal only, or one of each.
Author/Source:	Ellie Byrd

Facilitator Instructions

1) Explain the objectives of the exercise.
2) Distribute the High Hurdles worksheets (4 pages total) and review the information requested on each sheet.
3) Give participants 45 minutes to prepare their worksheets.
4) One at a time, ask each participant to present all of their High Hurdles worksheets. Allow 12 minutes per person.
   a. First, have them share their Past High Hurdles Worksheet, talk about past High Hurdles and describe how they dealt with them.
   b. Next, have them share their Current High Hurdles Worksheet and talk through their strategy for dealing with the challenges.
   c. There should be no interruptions while a person is presenting.
5) Optionally, if time permits you can allow a five minute Q&A period for Forum members to ask questions and/or share relevant experiences after each person's presentation.
6) Thank each person for sharing their worksheets before you move on to the next person.

Past High Hurdles Worksheet

Think back to the three biggest hurdles you've faced in your life. For each hurdle, describe the hurdle, how you dealt with it, and how it affected you.

Hurdle #1

Describe the hurdle. When did it happen?	
Describe how you dealt with it or overcame it. There may have been several strategies and actions involved.	
What did you learn from it or how did it change you?	

Hurdle #2

Describe the hurdle. When did it happen?	
Describe how you dealt with it or overcame it. There may have been several strategies and actions involved.	
What did you learn from it or how did it change you?	

Hurdle #3

Describe the hurdle. When did it happen?	
Describe how you dealt with it or overcame it. There may have been several strategies and actions involved.	
What did you learn from it or how did it change you?	

Answer two questions:

1) Is there a pattern or trend in the hurdles you have faced?

2) Is there a pattern or trend in how you have dealt with your hurdles?

Current High Hurdles Worksheet #1

Think of the top three hurdles you are facing today. Complete the worksheet below for one of the three hurdles.

Current Hurdle #1

❶ Define the Hurdle:

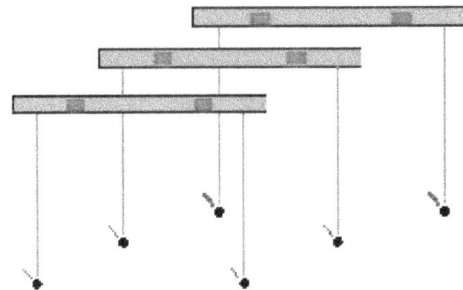

❷ Describe the current situation:

_____

_____

_____

_____

_____

_____

_____

❸ Describe the desired outcome:

_____

_____

_____

_____

❹ List the obstacles you will have to overcome:

_____

_____

_____

_____

_____

_____

_____

_____

_____

_____

❺ List the information, tools and resources you need::

_____

_____

_____

_____

_____

_____

_____

_____

_____

❻ List the action items you must take:

_____

_____

_____

_____

_____

_____

_____

_____

_____

Today's date _____   Goal date for resolution _____

Current High Hurdles Worksheet #2

Complete the worksheet below for the second hurdle.

Current Hurdle #2

❶ Define the Hurdle:

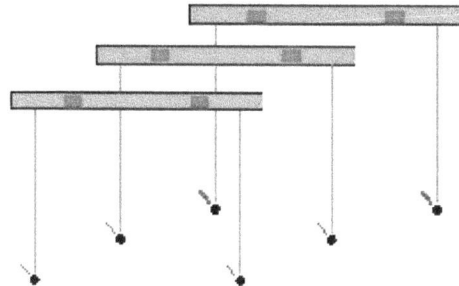

❷ Describe the current situation:

_____

_____

_____

_____

_____

_____

_____

❸ Describe the desired outcome:

_____

_____

_____

_____

❹ List the obstacles you will have to overcome:

_____

_____

_____

_____

_____

_____

_____

_____

_____

_____

❺ List the information, tools and resources you need::

_____

_____

_____

_____

_____

_____

_____

_____

_____

_____

_____

❻ List the action items you must take:

_____

_____

_____

_____

_____

_____

_____

_____

_____

_____

Today's date _____   Goal date for resolution _____

Current High Hurdles Worksheet #3

Complete the worksheet below for the third hurdle.

Current Hurdle #3

❶ Define the Hurdle:

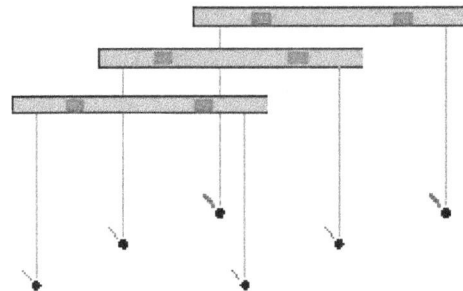

❷ Describe the current situation:

_____
_____
_____
_____
_____
_____
_____
_____

❸ Describe the desired outcome:

_____
_____
_____
_____

❹ List the obstacles you will have to overcome:

_____
_____
_____
_____
_____
_____
_____
_____
_____
_____

❺ List the information, tools and resources you need::

_____
_____
_____
_____
_____
_____
_____
_____
_____
_____

❻ List the action items you must take:

_____
_____
_____
_____
_____
_____
_____
_____
_____

Today's date _____   Goal date for resolution _____

Internal Experts

Internal Experts is an exercise whereby Forum members share their expertise and learn from each other. Everyone expands their knowledge on a variety of topics.

Objectives

- To give each member an opportunity to present on an area of their own expertise
- To learn from each other
- To learn more about each other

Facilitator Info

Depth Level:	Light
Facilitation Skills:	Basic
Estimated Time:	5 hours
Tools Needed:	Varies by presenter
Handouts:	None
Pre-work:	Each member prepares to give a 20-minute presentation on an area of expertise selected by the Forum.
Notes:	None
Author/Source:	Ellie Byrd

Facilitator Instructions

Before the retreat...

1) Several months before the retreat, ask each Forum member to identify three areas where they feel they have expertise, strong knowledge, or strong experience. A list of sample topics is provided here to get you started, but think out of the box on creative ideas.

2) Ask the other Forum members to vote on which of the person's three areas they would like to hear most. Choose one area for each person to give a topical presentation.

3) Each person prepares to give a 20-minute presentation on their area of expertise. If someone needs special equipment or room setup, be sure they arrange this in advance.

At the retreat...

At the retreat, each person gives their 20-minute presentation. Allow 10 minutes for questions and answers after each presentation.

Sample Topics

Raising capital
P/R for your company
Financial management
Unemployment claims
Collections and A/R procedures
Children with learning disabilities
Alcoholism
Playing poker
Living wills
Surviving cancer
Retirement planning
Commodities market
Sailing
Vintage cars
Classical music
Stamp collecting
Refinishing furniture
Negotiating
Meditation

Visualization – The Wall

Visualization – The Wall is an exercise in future thinking. Each person contemplates their future vision, obstacles that may block them and strategies to overcome the obstacles. At the end of the exercise, each person has more clarity on where they are going and how they can get there successfully.

Objectives

- To consider where you would like to be in five years
- To identify obstacles and solutions for overcoming the obstacles

Facilitator Info

Depth Level:	Medium
Facilitation Skills:	Light
Estimated Time:	2 hours
Tools Needed:	Paper, pens/pencils
Handouts:	None
Pre-work:	None
Notes:	Optionally, allow time for experience sharing after each person's presentation,
Author/Source:	YPO (Young Presidents' Organization)

Facilitator Instructions

1) Write the three questions in step 5 on a flipchart, but cover them up until you are ready.
2) Explain the objective of the exercise.
3) Ask everyone to think into the future. Think of what your life will be like 10 years from now if everything is going GREAT. Write down a few sentences that describe what this will be like. [Allow 3 minutes for them to write.]
4) Now, ask everyone to imagine that they are walking along a tranquil path toward this wonderful goal. Suddenly, your progress is blocked entirely by a wall. The wall is inhibiting you from reaching your goal!
5) Answer the following 3 questions. (Allow 10 minutes for this.)

   a. What does the wall represent in your life?
   b. How could you best overcome the wall?
   c. What is one thing you will do over the next 30 days to eliminate the wall?

6) Ask each person to talk about their dream of the future and the wall in front of them, then answer the three questions. Allow 7 minutes per person.
7) As a Forum, discuss how you could support each other to overcome your "walls".

Strength, Weakness, Joy and Pain

Strengths, Weakness, Joy and Pain is an introspective exercise where each member contemplates four questions, then shares their answers with the Forum. People learn more about themselves and more about each other.

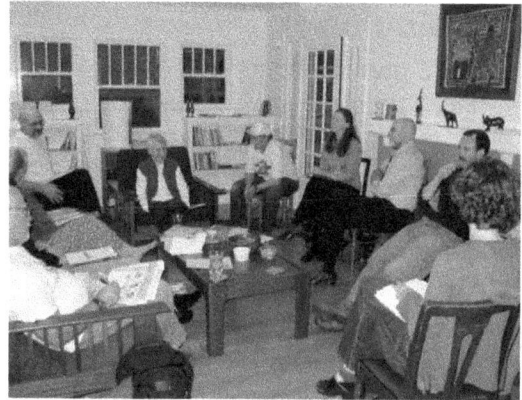

Objectives

- To consider our own strengths and weaknesses
- To think about what brings us joy and what causes us pain in our lives
- To learn more about each other and to learn from each other

Facilitator Info

Depth Level:	Medium
Facilitation Skills:	Light
Estimated Time:	90 minutes
Tools Needed:	Paper, pens/pencils
Handouts:	None
Pre-work:	None
Notes:	None
Author/Source:	YPO (Young Presidents' Organization)

Facilitator Instructions

1) Explain the objective of the exercise.
2) Ask everyone to think of the following four items and share one personal insight from each of the four areas.

   a. Strength – what is your greatest strength?

   b. Weakness – what is your biggest weakness?

   c. Joy – what brings you the most joy in your life?

   d. Pain – what causes you the most pain in your life?

3) Give people 10 minutes to think about what they would like to share and make notes on their paper.
4) Ask each person to share their four insights. There should be no discussion or questions during this exercise, only words of encouragement and support when appropriate. Everyone should listen intently as each person shares their four insights. Allow 7 minutes per person.

5 Mentors

The 5 Mentors exercise is an opportunity for each Forum member to deal with a difficult challenge by tapping into the wisdom of mentors. Through the exercise, people gain clarity on how to deal with a current challenge. Meanwhile, they learn from each other and about each other.

Objectives

- To consider who we perceive to be our mentors in life
- To gain insight on how our mentors would advise us to handle a current challenge
- To learn from each other

Facilitator Info

Depth Level:	Medium
Facilitation Skills:	Medium
Estimated Time:	2 hours
Tools Needed:	Pens/pencils
Handouts:	5 Mentors Worksheet
Pre-work:	None
Notes:	This exercise should be handwritten, not typed. According to the Journal of Cognitive Neuroscience and researchers Mueller and Oppenheimer, handwriting engages your brain, motor-skills and memory at a higher level than typing. By handwriting, the results will be deeper and more thoughtful.
Author/Source:	Unknown, adapted for Forum

Facilitator Instructions

1) Explain the objective of the exercise. Have a brief discussion on mentors – note that we all have mentors, even if the mentors themselves don't know it. We can get help from these people without talking to them, as demonstrated through this exercise.
2) Distribute the 5 Mentors Worksheet.
3) Think of five people who you consider to be good mentors or role models. These may be people who are living or dead. You may know them well or you may never have met them. Write their names at the top of the 5 Mentors Worksheet.
4) Now, think of a difficult challenge you are currently facing. This could be business, personal, spiritual, etc. Write a short paragraph at the top of the page to describe the challenge.
5) Next, assume that each of your five mentors is writing you a message with their thoughts on your challenge. Write down what they would say to you in their message. Allow 20 to 30 minutes for this part of the exercise.
6) Ask each person to share their 5 Mentors worksheet, reading what each mentor told them about their situation. Then, answer the following questions:
   a. Did you gain different insights from the five mentors? (If not, you may want to consider selecting different mentors and trying again.)
   b. Did this exercise bring new insights as to how you will approach this challenge?

5 Mentors Worksheet

My five mentors:

1. _____
2. _____
3. _____
4. _____
5. _____

A difficult challenge I am facing. (Write a short description.)

How my mentors would advise me on this challenge:

Mentor #1:	Advice:
Mentor #2:	Advice:
Mentor #3:	Advice:
Mentor #4:	Advice:
Mentor #5:	Advice:

Category 8

Building Depth

These exercises are the most intense of all the categories. Most of them require pre-work before the retreat and they all involve deep, introspective thinking. To be effective, these exercises require a high level of trust in confidentiality and a safe, non-judgmental environment.

Refer to Part 1 of this book, Planning Your Retreat, for information on how to facilitate exercises. Time estimates for individual exercises are based on an 8-person Forum. Adjust the time estimates as needed to accommodate the size of your Forum.

Category 8 Exercises

forumsherpa

Dealing with Pain

Dealing with Pain is an exercise that explores how people deal with painful situations. Forum members learn more about themselves and about each other by understanding how they deal with crisis and by sharing their experiences.

Objectives
- To reflect on difficult experiences in our life and how those experiences have shaped us
- To get to know our fellow Forum members better

Facilitator Info

Depth Level:	High
Facilitation Skills:	Advanced
Estimated Time:	2 hours
Tools Needed:	Paper, pens/pencils
Handouts:	Dealing with Pain Worksheet
Pre-work:	None
Notes:	A quiet, peaceful setting is a good location for this exercise.
Author/Source:	Bill Evans

Facilitator Instructions
1) Explain the stated objectives of this exercise.
2) Distribute the Dealing with Pain worksheet.
3) Walk through the five steps to be sure everyone understands the instructions.
4) Give people 30 minutes to complete the worksheet. It's fine for people to leave the room and go off on their own to do this.
5) When everyone returns, ask each person to share one of their experiences.

Debrief Questions
Ask people to contemplate and discuss the following questions:
   a) Are you more likely to reflect on painful events, or are you more likely to suppress them and not think about them?
   b) Were the painful events you wrote down within your control? In other words, could you have changed the situation and prevented it from turning into a painful event?

Dealing with Pain – Worksheet

1) When you are in pain, how do you usually react? (choose one)
   a) Talk to people immediately?
   b) Wait until the crisis is over and then tell people?
   c) Get through it the best way you can without help?

2) Write down the five most painful experiences in your life.

1.
2.
3.
4.
5.

3) Make a list of reasons why you have come to value these experiences.

Select one of the experiences that you would like to share with the Forum.

5-5-5 Factors of My Life

The 5-5-5 exercise guides Forum members to reflect on significant people, events and decisions that have affected their lives. By sharing these critical events with each other, people develop a better understanding of the inner self. This exercise is both introspective and enlightening.

Objectives

- To reflect on key factors of our life that impact who we are today
- To share intimate thoughts and feelings with the Forum
- To learn and support each other

Facilitator Info

Depth Level:	High
Facilitation Skills:	Advanced
Estimated Time:	3 hours
Tools Needed:	None
Handouts:	5-5-5 Factors Worksheets
Pre-work:	Complete the 5-5-5 Worksheets before the retreat.
Notes:	<ul><li>Optionally people can prepare a PowerPoint presentation and show it at the retreat as they talk through their factors.</li><li>A shorter variation of this exercise is 3-3-3. Share the top 3 most important factors in each category.</li><li>This exercise can become emotional for some people.</li></ul>
Author/Source:	Unknown, adapted for Forum

Facilitator Instructions

1) For advance preparation, ask everyone to prepare the 5-5-5 Worksheets. The worksheets includes the following:
   a) 5 most important **People** in my life
   b) 5 most important **Events** in my life
   c) 5 most important **Decisions** in my life
2) At the retreat, each person shares their 5-5-5 worksheet with the Forum.
3) After each person finishes their presentation, the Forum can ask questions, offer words of support and reflect on what they learned about the person.

5 – 5 – 5 Worksheet: People

Think back to the people who have had the most significant impact on your life. "People" could be a parent, a family member, a friend, a role model, a childhood teacher, a historical figure, etc. They can be living or dead, someone you know or someone you've never met. Identify the five most significant people and make notes about how they have affected your life and/or shaped you into who you are today.

5 People	Who is the person, how do you know them and why are they so important to you? How have they impacted your life? If you could say something to this person today, what would you like to say?
Person #1	
Person #2	
Person #3	
Person #4	
Person #5	

5 – 5 – 5 Worksheet: Events

What are the most significant events in your life thus far? Events could be the birth of a child, marriage, divorce, death of a loved one, life in a war-torn country, child-abuse, illness, etc. An event is something that happens to you. You may or may not be responsible for the happening of the event. Identify the five most significant events and make notes about how they have impacted your life and/or shaped you into who you are today.

5 Events	What is the event? What happened? When did it happen? How or why did it occur? What is its significance in your life?
Event #1	
Event #2	
Event #3	
Event #4	
Event #5	

5 – 5 – 5 Worksheet: Decisions

Think back to the most important decisions you have made in your life. Decisions could be starting your first business, getting married, choosing where you will live, leaving a country to escape oppression, etc. A decision is something that you have control over. It was a choice you made. It may have been a fork in the road, or a turning point in your life. Identify the five most important decisions you have made and make notes about the catalyst and impact of the decision.

5 Decisions	What was the decision you made? What other choices did you have? Why did you make the decision you made? If you could go back in time, would you make the same decision? How did the decision impact your life?
Decision #1	
Decision #2	
Decision #3	
Decision #4	
Decision #5	

Outcome-Based Thinking (OBT)

Outcome-Based Thinking is an exercise the guides Forum members through an introspective look at their hopes and dreams. Each person identifies actionable steps that will help them turn their dreams into reality.

Objectives

- To think about our goals and dreams
- To consider how we can turn our dreams into a reality
- To share our dreams with our Forum members and offer support to each other in achieving our goals

Facilitator Info

Depth Level:	High
Facilitation Skills:	Medium
Estimated Time:	2 hours
Tools Needed:	4 sheets of paper per person, pens/pencils
Handouts:	None
Pre-work:	None
Notes:	Much of this exercise is completed in silence, allowing people the opportunity to think, reflect, and plan.
Author/Source:	Francisco Puente

Facilitator Instructions

1) Explain the objectives of the exercise.
2) Distribute four sheets of paper to each person.
3) On the first sheet of paper, ask people to make a list of the dreams they have for their life in terms of the following items. There is no limit to the number of dreams they can list. Allow ten minutes for this.
   a. Relationships (family, friends, colleagues, others)
   b. Income
   c. Travel
   d. Professional development (career)
   e. Material possessions
   f. Other accomplishments
4) On the second sheet of paper, write one or two sentences about why you wish for each of your dreams. If a reason doesn't come to mind quickly, simply continue on to the next dream. Allow ten minutes for this.
5) For all the dreams that you couldn't think of a reason, these dreams will be sent to the "freezer" for storage, not to be dealt with in this exercise. For each of the remaining dreams, write a time frame in which you would like to accomplish these dreams; for example, six months, one year, five years, ten years, etc. Allow ten minutes for this.

Outcome-Based Thinking (OBT), continued

Facilitator Instructions, cont.

6) On the third sheet of paper, write one or two phrases that come between you and your dreams. Allow ten minutes for this. For example:
   a. Lose 20 pounds – I eat too many sweets, I don't like to exercise
   b. Earn $500,000 US a year – I'm not willing to give more time to the company
   c. Buy a house – I lack the confidence to do this; I spend too much money on other things.
7) On the fourth sheet of paper, divide the paper into 4 squares or sections. At the top of each square, write one of the four dreams that were most important to you and that are achievable in under a year. For example:
   a. Lose 10 pounds
   b. Pay for my house
   c. Read 20 books this year
   d. Spend more time with my children
8) In each quadrant, write the following information. Allow 20 minutes for this.
   a. Write all of the reasons why you absolutely should reach this goal or dream.
   b. Define the pain and how you would feel if you do not reach the goal or dream.
   c. Describe the pleasure and satisfaction you would feel if you did achieve each goal or dream.
   d. Write what you can do every day to drive you toward achieving each one of these dreams.

Ask each member to share their top four dreams, why they are important and what they are going to do in the coming months to achieve their dreams.

Exploring Your Mortality

Exploring Your Mortality is an exercise that presents six thought-provoking questions. Forum members work independently and introspectively to answer these questions. Then, everyone shares a one-page note with the Forum.

Objectives
- To think about our own mortality
- To reflect on potentially unspoken conversations
- To learn about our fellow Forum members

Facilitator Info

Depth Level:	High
Facilitation Skills:	Advanced
Estimated Time:	90 minutes
Tools Needed:	Paper, pens/pencils
Handouts:	Mortality Questions
Pre-work:	None
Notes:	Much of this exercise is completed in silence, allowing people the opportunity to think and reflect.
Author/Source:	Mo Fathelbab

Facilitator Instructions

1) Ask everyone to spend the next 25 minutes answering the Mortality Questions below.

Mortality Questions

1. When was the last time you feared for your life?
2. Do you believe in any sort of an afterlife?
3. If somehow you had proof that dispelled that belief, would you live your life differently? How?
4. Who do you think is the one person that would be most affected by your death?
5. Who is the one person whose death would most affect you? Why?
6. If you died tomorrow with no opportunity to communicate with anyone, what would you most regret not having communicated?

---

2) After answering these questions, prepare a one-page note to be sent to one person communicating whatever it is you would regret not having communicated. If no such regret exists, write a letter to be opened by your eldest child on his/her wedding day or graduation day. This should include the most important lessons you've learned in your life that you want to pass on and how you learned them.

3) Ask each person to read their note to the group. Also share if they are planning to give the note to the person.

Photo Gallery

In the Photo Gallery exercise, each Forum member shares photographs and talks about the most important people in their lives.

Objective

- To increase intimacy by allowing members to see into the most important people in their lives

Facilitator Info

Depth Level:	High
Facilitation Skills:	Medium
Estimated Time:	90 minutes
Tools Needed:	None
Handouts:	None
Pre-work:	Determine the 10 most important people in your life (alive or dead), and find a picture of each person. Put the pictures in order of importance.
Notes:	None
Author/Source:	Mo Fathelbab

Facilitator Instructions

1) Provide the instructions to the exercise at least two weeks in advance. Preparation time can require up to an hour.
2) Ask each member to determine the 10 most important people in their lives (dead or alive). Find a picture of each of these 10 people and put them in order of their importance to you.
3) At the retreat ensure that each member has prepared by organizing his/her photos in order from least important to most important.
4) Make sure that everyone is sitting within close proximity so that the pictures can be passed around easily. It's best not to sit around a table.
5) Once everyone is ready, each person starts by showing a picture of the 10th most important person and then passing it to the right while talking about what that person has meant to the member and what makes that person so significant. Each member continues on until completing the rest of the people on his/her list. Now it's time to move to the next person. Allow 10 minutes per person.
6) This exercise can be very emotional and is a good exercise to move a group to higher levels of depth.

Who Am I?

Who Am I? is a thought-provoking, introspective exercise that guides Forum members to consider how they became who they are today. People complete a comprehensive 4-page worksheet and share their answers at the retreat. People gain a new understanding of each other and feel more connected as a group.

Objectives

- To analyze who we are and the factors that have had the most influence in shaping our lives
- To reflect on three key aspects of life – parental influence, significant people and significant events

Facilitator Info

Depth Level:	High
Facilitation Skills:	Advanced
Estimated Time:	3 hours (20 minutes per person)
Tools Needed:	None
Handouts:	Who Am I? Worksheet (next 4 pages)
Pre-work:	Complete the worksheet before the retreat. This will take approximately two hours
Notes:	• The first person sets the tone for the others. If you are trying to achieve a high level of depth, start the exercise with someone who will be willing to share openly. • This exercise can be emotionally draining for some. Have tissues ready – there may be some tears. • Remember to stop for a break after about 90 minutes.
Author/Source:	Ellie Byrd

Facilitator Instructions

1) Distribute the "Who Am I?" worksheet several weeks before the retreat and ask everyone to complete it before the retreat.
2) Point out that the worksheet is several pages long and they may need to make several passes through the worksheet before they are comfortable. After completing all sections, answer the Summary Questions on the last page.

Facilitating the exercise

1) Each person should have their worksheets completed before you begin.
2) Explain the guidelines to everyone:
   a. Each person gets 20 minutes.
   b. There should be no interruptions while a person is presenting.
   c. Encourage everyone to share openly.
3) Begin with the first person, and continue with each person until finished.
4) If a person doesn't use their full time, allow for clarifying questions or experience sharing before moving to the next person.

Who Am I Worksheet

Significant Traits

Think about your parents and how they influenced your life, beginning in early childhood. Answer the following questions.

1) What were your parents' most prominent characteristics, traits and talents? (Note: you may use a parental figure if you didn't know one or both of your parents.) Here are some ideas to help you get started:

   -kind, patient, honest, sense of humor, humble, loyal, intelligent, creative, rigid, sturdy, intuitive, selfless, proud, angry, unhappy, depressed, optimistic, compulsive, artistic, manipulative, wise, risk-taker, energetic, alcoholic, religious, street-wise, lazy, loving.

	Father	Mother
Characteristics, traits and talents of your parents:		

2) Describe your parents' values. What were their priorities and what was most important to them?

3) Think of three examples of how your parents demonstrated their value system. These can be specific events or general behaviors.
   a)
   b)
   c)

4) Describe ways in which you are like your parents, i.e. which characteristics do you exhibit that you saw in them? Are you happy that you acquired these traits? Are there any traits that you wish you didn't have, that you struggle with, or that you fear you will develop?

5) Think about your own children, nieces and nephews. What values and characteristics would they say you exhibit by the way you live your life? What values would you like them to learn from you?

Who Am I Worksheet, continued

Significant People

Think of the five people in your life who have had the greatest positive impact on you. These people may be living or dead, or someone you've never met. Answer these questions for each of the five people.

Question	1	2	3	4	5
Who is this person and what was their relationship to you? When and how did you know them (or know of them)?					
What did you learn from them?					
What most impressed you about them?					
If you could say something to this person today, what would it be?					

Who Am I Worksheet, continued

Significant Events

Think of three key life-changing events in your life. This could be a major decision or a fork in the road that took you down one path versus another, it could be an unexpected event that took you by surprise and changed your life forever, or it could be any event that had a significant impact on you. Answer these questions for each of the three events.

Question	1	2	3
Describe the background and the event itself.			
How did the event change your life?			
If you could go back in time, is there anything you would have done differently before, during or after this event?			

Who Am I Worksheet, continued

Summary Questions

After completing the "Who Am I?" worksheets, answer the following questions.

1) What did you learn about yourself as you worked on this exercise?

2) What changes would you like to make in your life as a result of reflecting on these significant events and people?

3) What are specific action items that you would like to take moving forward?

Brown Bag

The Brown Bag exercise is an opportunity for Forum members to contemplate what is most important in their lives, creating a "top ten" list. People select an object to represent each item on their top ten list, place them in a brown paper bag and bring the bag to the retreat. Everyone shares the items in their brown bag at the retreat.

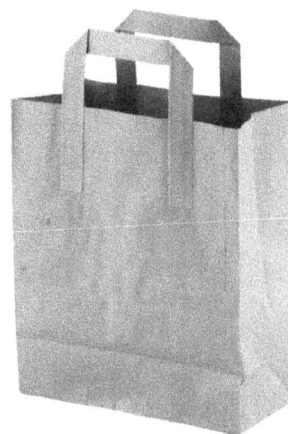

Objectives

- To reflect on our lives and the things that are the most meaningful and important to us
- To have an opportunity for members to share their own life experiences and values, and to learn more about each other

Facilitator Info

Depth Level:	High
Facilitation Skills:	Medium
Estimated Time:	2 hours, 15 minutes (15 minutes per person)
Tools Needed:	None
Handouts:	Brown Bag Worksheet
Pre-work:	Identify 10 items to signify the 10 most important things in your life. Bring them to the retreat in a brown bag.
Notes:	• Decide when and where you will do the exercise. This is a great exercise for after dinner, around the fire, or in a comfortable setting. Sit in a circle on the floor or in comfortable chairs. No table! • The first person sets the tone for the others. If you are trying to achieve a high level of depth, start the exercise with someone who will be willing to share deeply and openly. • Have tissues ready – this exercise often results in some tears. • Remember to stop for a break after about 90 minutes.
Author/Source:	Unknown, adapted for Forum

Facilitator Instructions

1) Several weeks before the retreat, explain the purpose of the exercise and distribute the Brown Bag worksheet.
2) Each person should have their brown bag with them before you begin the exercise.
3) Explain the guidelines to everyone:
   a. Encourage everyone to share openly.
   b. There should be no interruptions while a person is presenting their 10 items. Show the 10th most important item first and talk about its significance. Then show the 9th, 8th, 7th, and so on, discussing each item as you go. The last item to show it the most important one.
   c. It's fine for people to pass items around the room (e.g. a photograph, memento, etc.), but wait until all items circulate back to the presenter before you continue to the next person's presentation
   d. Each person gets 15 minutes.

Brown Bag Worksheet

This is an exercise that often leads Forums to a new level of depth, understanding, and appreciation. Please take plenty of time to think carefully about the things in your life that are the most important to you, and about the objects you select to represent them.

1) Think of ten objects that represent the ten most important things in your life. Here are some examples:

> - Family – bring a picture of your family
> - Business – bring a business card
> - Playing golf – bring a golf ball
> - Weight Watcher's gold key – signifies losing weight and achieving your goal
> - Your father's Bible – he instilled his values and principles in you when you were growing up, and your mother gave you his Bible after he died
> - Cancelled check from when you finally paid off your first business loan
> - Copy of the mortgage deed when you bought your first house
> - An old shoe that your dog chewed up, but it was his favorite toy

2) Prioritize these items in order of their importance:

Priority	Important Thing	Object / Significance
1		
2		
3		
4		
5		
6		
7		
8		
9		
10		

3) Gather the items and bring them with you in a brown paper bag to the retreat.

At the Retreat...
Each person will take turns revealing the items in their "brown bag" and discussing why they are so important to them.

Lifeline

The Lifeline is an introspective, thought-provoking exercise. Forum members think of the significant events in their life and plot them on a chronological chart, positioning each item as a high point, low point or somewhere in between. After plotting all of the significant points, the points are connected by a line which becomes the "life line".

Objectives

- To reflect on our lives and the events that have shaped us into who we are today
- To gain a new understanding of our fellow Forum members
- To share the high points and low points of our lives with our Forum members
- To have an opportunity for all Forum members to share their life experiences and values

Facilitator Info

Depth Level:	High
Facilitation Skills:	Advanced
Estimated Time:	3 hours (20 minutes per person)
Tools Needed:	None
Handouts:	Lifeline Worksheet
Pre-work:	Complete the Lifeline Worksheet before the retreat
Notes:	• This is a popular exercise for new Forums. Many Forums repeat the exercise when new members join the Forum. • Decide when and where you will do the exercise. This is a great exercise for after dinner, around the fire, or in a comfortable setting. Sit in a circle on the floor in comfortable chairs. No table! • The first person sets the tone for the others. If you are trying to achieve a high level of depth, start the exercise with someone who will be willing to share deeply and openly. • Remember to stop for a break after about 90 minutes.
Author/Source:	Unknown, adapted for Forum

Facilitator Instructions

1) Several weeks before the retreat, explain the purpose of the exercise and distribute the Lifeline worksheet.
2) Each person must complete their Lifeline Worksheet before the exercise begins.
3) Explain the guidelines to everyone:
   a. Each person gets 20 minutes.
   b. There should be no interruptions while a person is talking.
   c. Encourage everyone to share openly.
   d. Begin with the first person, and continue with each person until finished.
4) After each person finished their presentation, thank them for sharing with the group, then move to the next person.

Lifeline, continued

Lifeline Variations

- Bring photographs to show during your lifeline (submitted by Nancy Leach, Nashville).
- Create a "business only" lifeline.
- Create a "family only" lifeline.
- Create a "spiritual only" lifeline.
- Create a lifeline of your childhood only – up to age 18. Talk about your parents, where did you live, etc. (submitted by Jennifer Mackin)
- Create a lifeline of key decisions/crossroads in your life.
- Create a future lifeline; for example, what will happen between now and the end of your life.
- Give each person one hour to present their lifeline. This enables people to go into much more depth.

Lifeline Worksheet

Think of your life from the day you were born until today. Think of the high points, the low points, the key decisions, significant events and the people that shaped your life. Plot each of these as points on the chart below. The ages of your life are shown at the center line in 5-year increments. Plot high point in the upper section and low points in the lower section, relative to how high or low they were. Connect the dots to form your "life line".

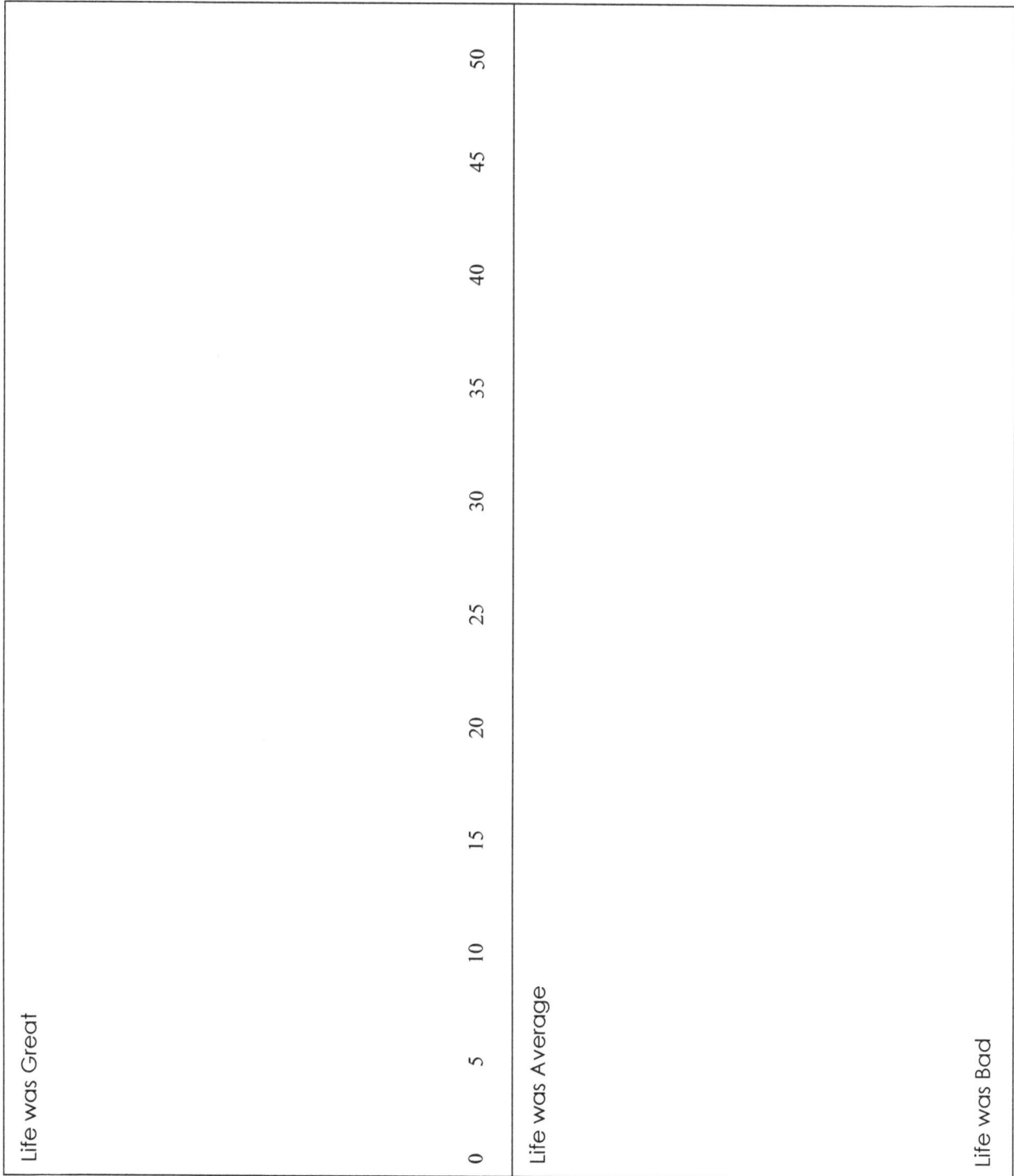

Life was Great

Life was Average

0   5   10   15   20   25   30   35   40   45   50

Life was Bad

Letter from the Other Side

Letter from the Other Side is a powerful exercise that takes Forum members to a high and intense level of depth. Forum members imagine a scenario of mortality and visualize writing a letter to someone to say goodbye. This is an emotional exercise that often results in a strong bonding experience for the Forum.

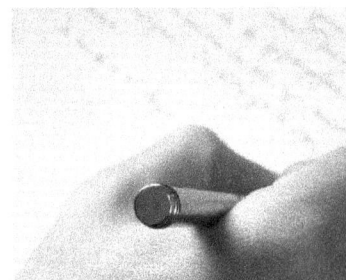

Objectives

- To think about our own mortality, and the message we would want our families to have from us
- To share openly with each other
- To get to know each other more intimately and gain a new understanding of each other

Facilitator Info

Depth Level:	High
Facilitation Skills:	Advanced
Estimated Time:	2 hours, 30 minutes (10 minutes per person)
Tools Needed:	Pens/pencils
Handouts:	Blank paper
Pre-work:	None
Notes:	• Don't tell the Forum in advance that they will be doing this exercise. • This exercise can become emotional. Have tissues ready.
Author/Source:	David Steel

Facilitator Instructions

1) Explain the objectives of the exercise.
2) Read the following description of how to complete the exercise.

> Imagine that we are all traveling home from the retreat tomorrow and something terrible happens en route. None of us make it home. Imagine that you have been given an amazing gift - you can write a letter to someone (spouse, child, friend, relative) telling them your thoughts and feelings. Think of your hopes for them. Think of what you would like them to know that you never told them. You can also ask them to deliver a message to other people for you. Write these thoughts in a letter to this person.

3) Give everyone 30 minutes to write their letter.
4) Explain the guidelines to everyone:
   a. Remind everyone that what is said in the room stays in the room.
   b. Each person gets 15 minutes.
   c. There should be no interruptions while a person is talking.
   d. Encourage everyone to share openly.
   e. Begin with the first person, and continue with each person until finished.
5) Ask each person to read their letter. Then have each person reflect on how it felt to write the letter, what they learned about themselves, and what they might want to do differently.
6) After each person finishes reading their letter, thank them for sharing with the group, then move to the next person.

Pass It On

Pass it On is a thought-provoking, introspective exercise that guides Forum members through a process of self-discovery. Preparation is required, and the exercise builds on the preparatory work at the retreat.

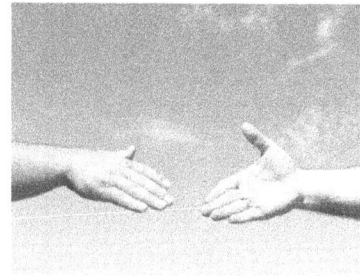

Objectives

- To think about our relationships with key people in our lives
- To share openly with each other
- To gain a new understanding of our fellow Forum members

Facilitator Info

Depth Level:	High
Facilitation Skills:	Advanced
Estimated Time:	3 hours
Tools Needed:	Paper, pens/pencils
Handouts:	None
Pre-work:	Each member writes a letter that they wish one of their parents, a spouse or a child would have written to them.
Notes:	Make sure you have plenty of lined paper on hand. Those who are more comfortable typing can use their laptop.
Author/Source:	YPO (Young Presidents' Organization)

Facilitator Instructions

1) Several weeks before the retreat, explain the objective of the exercise and the pre-work.
2) The pre-work consists of writing a fictitious letter before the retreat. This is to be a letter that they wish their mother, father, spouse or child would have written to them.
3) At the retreat, ask each member to read their letter to the Forum, adding any necessary information to understand the importance and perspective. There should be no interruptions while a person is reading.
4) Next, give everyone two hours to compose a letter that they would like to send as a result of the first, fictitious letter. Note that the second letter does not have to be sent to the same person that the member wished to receive the first letter from, but there should be a connection. For example, if the member wishes he had received a letter from a deceased parent, he may want to write a similar letter to his child.
5) When everyone has finished writing their letter, each person reads the second letter to the Forum.

Debrief Questions

As a group, discuss the following questions.

a) How did you feel as you were writing the first letter?
b) How did you feel as you were writing the second letter?
c) Will you actually give the second letter to the person? Why or why not?
d) What did you learn about yourself and your relationships as you worked on this exercise?

Future Flight

Future Flight is a visualization exercise, projecting what will happen over the next ten years. Forum members visualize a conversation with someone ten years in the future and write out the key points they anticipate in their life.

Objectives

- To think about our relationships with key people in our lives
- To share openly with each other
- To get to know our fellow Forum members better and gain new understanding of each other's hopes and dreams

Facilitator Info

Depth Level:	High
Facilitation Skills:	Advanced
Estimated Time:	2 hours
Tools Needed:	Paper, pens/pencils
Handouts:	None
Pre-work:	None
Notes:	A quiet, peaceful location is ideal for people to write their Future Flight conversation.
Author/Source:	Ellie Byrd

Facilitator Instructions

1) Read the instructions to everyone.

> Imagine it is 10 years from today, 10 years into the future, so the year is _____. You board a plane and take your seat, only to realize that one of your fellow Forum members who moved away and left the Forum 10 years ago is seated next to you! You are elated to connect again because you have lost touch over the years.
>
> They want to know everything about your life. What has happened in the last 10 years? How is your family? How are your children? How is your business? How is the Forum?
>
> Write down what you will tell them, looking back on the 10 year time span as if it has already happened.

2) Give everyone paper and pencils and let them write. It will be almost like writing a letter – a one-sided conversation with this person who you once knew so well and cared for as a fellow Forum member. Allow 45 minutes for this. (People can leave the room and go off on their own to write.)

Future Flight, continued

Facilitator Instructions, continued

3) Bring everyone back together.
4) One by one, ask each person to read their conversational letter. There should be no interruptions while someone is reading.
5) After a person finishes reading, allow 5 minutes for questions and answers.
6) Then, continue to the next person.

Debrief Questions

As a group, discuss the following questions.

a) How did it feel to do this exercise?
b) How likely is it that the events in the letter will come true?
c) What is one thing that each person could do to achieve one of the outcomes they desire?

Category 9
Retreat Closers

Use these exercises at the end of the retreat to review the retreat, reflect on events, and bring the retreat to a comfortable close.

Refer to Part 1 of this book, Planning Your Retreat, for information on how to facilitate exercises. Time estimates for individual exercises are based on an 8-person Forum. Adjust the time estimates as needed to accommodate the size of your Forum.

Category 9 Exercises

forumsherpa

Annual Forum Goals

The Annual Forum Goals exercise is an opportunity for the Forum to think proactively about what they want to accomplish as a group during the coming year. Three specific goals are identified.

Objectives

- To collectively select three goals that the Forum will strive to accomplish over the coming year
- To consider how the Forum can continue to build strength and provide value to its members

Facilitator Info

Depth Level:	Medium
Facilitation Skills:	Medium
Estimated Time:	30 minutes
Tools Needed:	Flipchart, markers
Handouts:	None
Pre-work:	None
Notes:	This exercise is a good way to end the retreat and keep the momentum moving forward.
Author/Source:	Ellie Byrd

Facilitator Instructions

1) Introduce the objectives of the exercise.
2) On a flipchart, begin listing ideas of possible goals that the Forum could strive to achieve over the coming year. Keep in mind that goals should be specific, measurable, and realistic. Here are some ideas to get you started:
   - All members meet with each member individually during the year.
   - All members attend an educational event together.
   - Add one new member.
   - Don't lose any members.
   - Increase our level of Forum satisfaction to 9 or higher (on a scale of 10).
   - Improve attendance and decrease absences to two or less for the entire year for all members.
   - Every member helps every other member at least once during the year.
   - Each member increases their company revenues by 10%.
3) Scribe all the ideas on flipchart paper.
4) Ask each member to vote for their top three goals. They can do this by taking a marker and placing a tick mark next to their top three choices.
5) Take the top five goals and write them on a new sheet.
6) Engage in a healthy discussion of the benefits of each goal and the risks of not achieving the goal.
7) Ask people to come up one more time and vote for their top three favorite goals.
8) The three choices that receive the most votes become the three annual Forum goals for the year.
9) Consider listing these three goals at the top of every Forum meeting agenda over the coming year.

Appreciation

The Appreciation exercise is an opportunity for everyone to reflect on the positive aspects of the retreat and thank each person for their contribution.

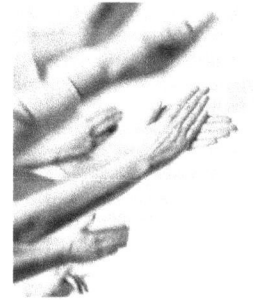

Objectives

- To reflect on the retreat experience
- To express appreciation to our fellow Forum members for contributions each person made during the retreat
- To learn how other members of the Forum perceive our own contribution to the retreat

Facilitator Info

Depth Level:	Medium
Facilitation Skills:	Basic
Estimated Time:	20 minutes
Tools Needed:	Flipchart, markers
Handouts:	None
Pre-work:	None
Notes:	• This exercise is a good way to end the retreat on a positive note. • There are two variations on this exercise – see Written Appreciation and Quick Appreciation.
Author/Source:	"Retreats That Work", adapted for Forum

Facilitator Instructions

1) Have the group sit in a circle.
2) Explain that this exercise is an opportunity to reflect on the retreat, and consider how each member of the Forum contributed to the retreat. This is an opportunity to express your appreciation to each person for their contribution.
3) Begin by demonstrating.
   a. Select one person, and provide your own personal thoughts on how this person contributed to the retreat. Thank them for their contribution.
   b. Continue around the room in a circle and ask the other Forum members to express their thanks to this person and describe how they contributed to the event.
4) Move to the next person and repeat the exercise, going around the room and having each member share their appreciation for how this person contributed to the retreat.
5) Repeat the process for everyone in the Forum.
6) After everyone has been appreciated by everyone else, the exercise ends.

Written Appreciation

The Written Appreciation exercise is an opportunity for Forum members to write a note of thanks to each other person in the Forum, regarding the value they bring to the Forum.

Objectives

- To reflect on the positive attributes of our fellow Forum members
- To express appreciation to each other for something of value that each person brings to the Forum
- To receive a written list from our Forum members about the value they feel we bring to the Forum

Facilitator Info

Depth Level:	Medium
Facilitation Skills:	Basic
Estimated Time:	30 minutes
Tools Needed:	Blank paper and pens/pencils
Handouts:	None
Pre-work:	None
Notes:	• This exercise is a good way to end the retreat on a positive note. • A shorter version of the exercise is also available (see Quick Appreciation).
Author/Source:	Unknown, adapted for Forum

Facilitator Instructions

1) Hand out one sheet of paper to each person.
2) Introduce the exercise as an opportunity to tell fellow members what we appreciate about them. We spend several hours together at our monthly meetings, and several days together on our annual retreat, but we don't often take the time to thank each other or complement each other.
3) Ask each person to write their name at the top of their paper.
4) Pass their paper to the left, one person.
5) Ask everyone to look at the page in front of them and write down a compliment or a thank you to the person whose name is at the top of the page.
6) Pass the paper to the left again. Again, write a compliment or a thank you to this person.
7) Continue passing the papers around. Eventually your own paper will come back to you, filled with compliments and thanks from your fellow Forum members.

Quick Appreciation

Quick Appreciation is a fast (5 minute) exercise that helps the Forum to end the retreat on a positive note. People reflect on the value each person brings to the Forum.

Objectives

- To express appreciation to another Forum member for the value they bring to the Forum
- To receive a word of appreciation from a fellow Forum member

Facilitator Info

Depth Level:	Light
Facilitation Skills:	Basic
Estimated Time:	5 minutes
Tools Needed:	None
Handouts:	None
Pre-work:	None
Notes:	• This exercise is designed to make a comment on the person's value to the Forum. A variation is to make a comment on how the person contributed to the success of this retreat. • This exercise is a good way to end the retreat on a positive note.
Author/Source:	Unknown, adapted for Forum

Facilitator Instructions

1) Introduce the exercise as an opportunity to express thanks to each other.
2) Explain that you will go around the room in a circle and each person will give a compliment to the person on their left.
3) Start by example, and give a compliment to the person on your left.
4) This person then turns to their left and gives a compliment to the person sitting next to them. And so on.
5) The exercise continues until the last person gives a compliment to you.

Letter to Myself

Letter to Myself is an exercise that helps Forum members think about the overall retreat and the action steps they would like to take after the retreat. Each person puts their action steps in writing and seals their letter in an envelope. Later, the letters are sent back to the person who wrote them, reminding each person of their commitments.

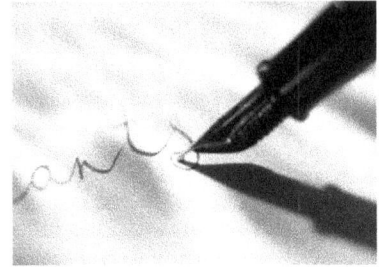

Objectives

- To take quiet time to contemplate actionable steps that each person wants to take after the retreat
- To write a letter to ourselves about commitments we have made during the retreat
- To increase our level of commitment to take action

Facilitator Info

Depth Level:	Light
Facilitation Skills:	Basic
Estimated Time:	30 minutes
Tools Needed:	Stationary, pens/pencils, envelopes
Handouts:	None
Pre-work:	None
Notes:	None
Author/Source:	"Retreats That Work", adapted for Forum

Facilitator Instructions

1) Distribute the stationary and envelopes to the Forum members.
2) Introduce the activity: "Please write a letter to yourself that summarizes what you commit to do differently as a result of this retreat. Be as specific as possible in making your commitments."
   a. What will you do?
   b. By what date will you do it?
   c. How will you know when you have done it?
3) Tell everyone that you will send the letters to them to remind them of their commitment in approximately two weeks. Be sure they know that the contents of their envelope will remain sealed and nobody will see what they write.
4) Give participants ten minutes to write their letters and seal them in the envelopes.
5) Ask them to write their names and addresses on their envelopes. (They can decide if they prefer to use their office address or home address)
6) Collect the letters. Send out the letters in two weeks.

Retreat Evaluation #1 and #2

Retreat evaluations are an opportunity for people to express their thoughts and feelings about the retreat. By collecting feedback immediately after the retreat, the Forum can analyze the success of the current retreat while maintaining helpful data for planning the next retreat.

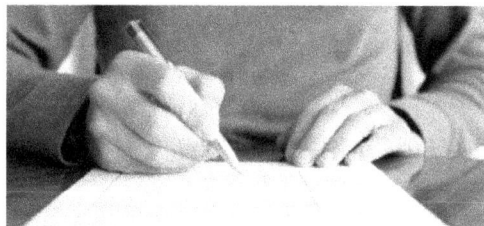

Objectives

- To reflect on the retreat, including the exercises, activities, and a variety of factors
- To express thoughts, opinions, ideas, complaints, suggestions, compliments and take-away value
- To secure a written record of people's impressions of the retreat – useful for a debrief at the next Forum meeting and helpful for making the plan for next year's retreat

Facilitator Info

Depth Level:	Light
Facilitation Skills:	Basic
Estimated Time:	15 minutes
Tools Needed:	Pens/pencils
Handouts:	Evaluation Form #1 or #2 (select one, or make up your own!)
Pre-work:	None
Notes:	<ul><li>Ideally, this exercise is done immediately after the retreat, before people start to leave.</li><li>The evaluation can be conducted online which simplifies the compilation process. However, it can cause complications if everyone doesn't respond.</li><li>Some Forums like to repeat the retreat evaluation about three months after the retreat to gauge the longer lasting impact of the retreat.</li></ul>
Author/Source:	Ellie Byrd

Facilitator Instructions

1) Select which Retreat Evaluation form you will use, or make up your own.
2) Explain the importance of collecting everyone's thoughts while the retreat is still fresh in their minds.
3) Hand out the Retreat Evaluation form and ask each person to complete it candidly. Names are optional.
4) Collect the forms.
5) Later, compile the results, and at the next Forum meeting, share the results.
6) Save the results and key discussion points to assist with planning the retreat next year.

Retreat Evaluation #1

Surveys are one way for us to assess retreat performance and effectiveness. Your response will help us plan next year's retreat to be an even better experience.

This will take less than 5 minutes! Please do it now!

Please rate your retreat experience on each of the following.

	1	2	3	4	5	6	7	8	9	10
Attendance of entire group										
Punctuality of members at sessions										
Knowledge of other members										
Experience sharing of other members										
Willingness of members to help with retreat planning										
Development of trust										
Pre-preparation of participants										
Exercises – depth										
Exercises – diversity										
Openness of the Forum										
Moderator – leadership										
Moderator – sensitivity as needed										
Facilitator (if applicable)										
Retreat – planning										
Retreat – organization										
Retreat – take away value										
Achievement of retreat objectives										

Comments:

Please share anything else you like. Comments, complaints, suggestions, and ideas are welcome!

_____

_____

_____

_____

_____

_____

Retreat Evaluation #2

Surveys are one way for us to assess retreat performance and effectiveness. Your response will help us plan next year's retreat to be an even better experience.

1) What three things did you like most about the retreat?

2) What three things could be changed to improve the next retreat?

3) In your opinion, the length of the retreat was... (circle one)

    a) too short
    b) about right
    c) too long

4) Please rate each retreat exercise on a scale of 1 to 10 (1 is not helpful, 10 is very valuable):

    a) Exercise #1 (insert title):   1 2 3 4 5 6 7 8 9 10
    b) Exercise #2 (insert title):   1 2 3 4 5 6 7 8 9 10
    c) Exercise #3 (insert title):   1 2 3 4 5 6 7 8 9 10
    d) Exercise #4 (insert title):   1 2 3 4 5 6 7 8 9 10
    e) Exercise #5 (insert title):   1 2 3 4 5 6 7 8 9 10
    f) Exercise #6 (insert title):   1 2 3 4 5 6 7 8 9 10
    g) Exercise #7 (insert title):   1 2 3 4 5 6 7 8 9 10

5) Do you have any comments on specific exercises?

6) What exercises / activities would you like to see on the next retreat?

7) Do you feel the retreat goals were met? Circle your answer on a scale of 1 to 10.
    a) Retreat goals met: 1 2 3 4 5 6 7 8 9 10

8) Please provide comments about how well retreat goals were met for you or why they were not.

Take-Away Value

Take-away value is an exercise that guides Forum members to think about what they learned on the retreat, the follow-up actions they want to take and any changes the Forum might like to make.

Objectives

- To reflect on the retreat experience
- To enable each person to identify what they learned
- To consider the potential take-away value of the retreat – for the individual Forum members and for the group as a whole

Facilitator Info

Depth Level:	Medium
Facilitation Skills:	Basic
Estimated Time:	30 minutes
Tools Needed:	Post-it Notes, pens/pencils, three sheets of flipchart paper, with one question from the list below written at the top of each page.
Handouts:	None
Pre-work:	None
Notes:	None
Author/Source:	"Retreat That Work", adapted for Forum

Facilitator Instructions

1) Introduce the activity. "You've been away from your usual routine for X days. Reflect on this time as an investment in making positive changes."
2) Distribute Post-it Notes to each person.
3) Ask each person to write the answer to these three questions on three separate Post-It Notes.

> 1. One of the most important things I learned on this retreat is...
>
> 2. One thing that I would like to personally commit to doing as a result of this retreat is...
>
> 3. One thing I would like the Forum to commit to doing differently as a result of this retreat is...

4) Start with the first question. Go around the room and ask each person to read their answer, and then post their note on the appropriate flipchart page. People should not comment on other people's responses.
5) Continue to the second question. Have everyone read and post their note. Again, hold comments on other people's responses.
6) Continue to the third question. Have everyone read and post their note. Because the third question involves the entire group, engage in a brief discussion on how people feel about the ideas presented. Don't delve too deeply into the issue – this is intended to be a closing exercise. If necessary, commit to continuing the discussion at your next Forum meeting.
7) Remember to capture these thoughts on paper for future discussion.

Honoring Each Other

Honoring Each Other is a fun, creative and meaningful exercise. At the beginning of the retreat, Forum members are randomly given the name of another Forum member. At the end of the retreat, each person "honors" the person whose name they drew.

Objective

- To give and receive appreciation from our fellow Forum members

Facilitator Info

Depth Level:	Medium
Facilitation Skills:	Basic
Estimated Time:	5 minutes at beginning of retreat +1 hour at end of retreat
Tools Needed:	Anything available without purchase
Handouts:	Copies of Written Instruction
Pre-work:	None
Notes:	This exercise works extremely well with a mature Forum that has been together for many years. Members find inventive, creative ways of honoring each other. The final ceremony is fantastic – filled with creativity, gratitude and (sometimes) tears.
Author/Source:	Brigid Goldberg

Facilitator Instructions

At the beginning of the retreat...

1) Write down each person's name on a piece of paper. Place all names in a container.
2) Have each person draw out a name (not their own) and keep the name secret.
3) Explain that at the end of the retreat, each person will have the opportunity to honor the person whose name they have selected.
4) Provide copies of the Written Instructions (below). You will need to allot time at the final retreat session to do the ceremony.

At the end of the retreat...

5) Let each person give their presentation to the member whose name they drew.

Honoring Each Other, continued

Written Instructions

At the end of the retreat, we will have an Honoring Ceremony.

You have drawn the name of one of your fellow Forum members. You can honor this person in any way you choose.

Think about the following:

1) What have you learned from this person over the course of your time together?

2) What has struck you about this person?

3) What does he or she bring to the Forum, and to the world, that is unique and special?

Tangible representations have a lasting impact. You can use any materials already available to you in the process, but purchases are not allowed.

Please don't reveal whom you are honoring until the end of the retreat!

Expectations and Outcomes

Expectations and Outcomes is an exercise that asks each Forum member to write private notes about what they expect to get out of the retreat, then review their notes at the end of the retreat for comparison. Members reflect on whether their expectations were met and whether their perceptions have changed during the retreat.

Objectives

- To begin the retreat by having Forum members think about what they would like to get out of the retreat
- To end the retreat by reflection on how well their expectations were met

Facilitator Info

Depth Level:	Light
Facilitation Skills:	Basic
Estimated Time:	5 minutes
Tools Needed:	3 x 5 cards, pens/pencils and envelopes for each person, flipchart, markers
Handouts:	None
Pre-work:	None
Notes:	None
Author/Source:	"Retreats That Work", adapted for Forum

Facilitator Instructions, Part One

Part one occurs at the beginning of the retreat.

1) On the flipchart, write down the following three questions.
    a) The main thing I would like to get out of this retreat is...
    b) One thing I am concerned about is...
    c) One thing I would like to learn during this retreat is...
2) Give a 3 x 5 card to each person.
3) Ask them to answer these three questions on their card. Tell them to be completely honest and write down the first thing that comes to mind. Nobody will see their card but them.
4) Give everyone about five minutes to answer the three questions.
5) Give each person an envelope. Ask them to put their card inside the envelope, seal it and write their name on the outside.
6) Collect the envelopes until the end of the retreat when you will return the envelopes.

Expectations & Outcomes, continued

Facilitator Instructions, Part Two

Part two occurs at the end of the retreat.

1) At the end of the retreat, give everyone their envelope back.
2) Have everyone open their envelope and read their thoughts.
3) Ask them to reflect on whether their expectations were met. Also, consider how their perspective may have changed from the beginning of the retreat until the end.
4) Ask for volunteers who would like to share their insights.

Index

About the Author

Ellie Byrd is the Founder and CEO of ForumSherpa, Inc., an executive leadership organization that provides tools and services for high-functioning peer teams called Forums. As a Forum specialist, Ellie spends the majority of her time traveling the world and working with teams of CEO's, Presidents, entrepreneurs and leadership teams.

Ellie is an experienced facilitator who blends structured Forum best practices with warmth and trust. She is skilled at recognizing group and individual behaviors and helping teams forge a path to constructive meetings, deep relationships and strong take-away value.

To date, Ellie is credited with having developed hundreds of training programs and online training simulations, as well as having personally trained tens of thousands of people. She has delivered leadership communication programs to thousands of CEO's around the globe and is a frequent speaker on group dynamics and accountability at conferences and universities.

Ellie has introduced the Forum concept into several vertical markets, including senior military officers, church pastors, C-level executives and MBA Entrepreneur students. Throughout her career, Ellie has founded several successful companies, authored multiple books and released a CD as a concert pianist. In her spare time, Ellie enjoys playing the piano at conferences, churches and elder-care facilities, blending her passion for music with a message of joyful perseverance.

Bibliography

The following sources are acknowledged for specific exercises in this book. These exercises were adapted for Forums and modified to align with ForumSherpa's standard exercise format.

Books with Retreat Exercises

"All Together Now"
by Lorraine L. Ukens
Jossey-Bass/Pfieffer, San Francisco, CA, 1999

"Building Team Spirit"
by Barry Heermann
McGraw-Hill Companies, United States, 1997

"CEO Tools"
by Kraig Kramers
Gandy Dancer Press, United States, 2002

"Retreats That Work"
by Sheila Campbell, Merianne Liteman and Steve Sugar
Jossey-Bass/Pfeiffer, San Francisco, CA, 2003

"Team Games for Trainers"
by Carolyn Nilson
McGraw-Hill, Inc, New York, NY, 1993

Books with Ice Breakers / Communication Starters

"If... Questions for the Soul"
by Evelyn McFarlane & James Saywell
Villard Books, New York, NY, 1998

"The Book of Questions"
by Gregory Stock, Ph.D.
Workman Publishing Company Inc, New York, NY, 1987

"BrainTicklers II" (Questions for CEOs)
by Brainticklers Publishing
Boulder, Colorado, 2001

The "Ungame" (set of cards with questions)
by Rhea Zakich
www.talicor.com

Want More Exercises?

Take a look at ForumSherpa's Resource Center – a rapidly growing community of people seeking high quality exercises for a variety of events.

- New exercises added every month
- Contributed from a variety of sources
- Searchable by category, keywords, author, objectives, length, pre-work
- Professionally compiled with facilitator instructions
- Includes interactive worksheets (where applicable)
- A powerful, new resource for Moderators and Facilitators

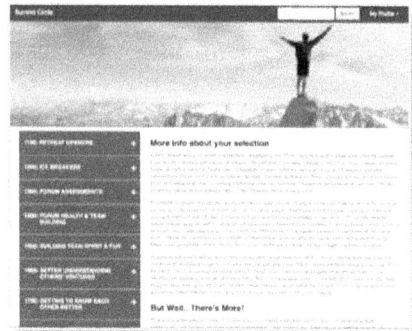

Visit **www.forumsherpa.com/resource-center** for more information!

Want Help Planning Your Retreat?

For Forums that are on a budget and/or want to facilitate their own retreat, ForumSherpa's Self-Facilitated Retreat Builder™ service is the perfect solution!

The process begins with a phone meeting with one of our certified facilitators. We discuss a variety of topics –the composition of your Forum, the objectives of the retreat, the retreat length and location, Forum history, etc. Based on the conversation and an online survey of your Forum members, we plan your retreat agenda and exercises. We compile your materials into a professional workbook and we coach you through how to facilitate the retreat on your own. After the retreat, we run a post-retreat evaluation for review and future reference.

Visit **www.forumsherpa.com/retreats-self-facilitated** for more information.

Want a Certified Sherpa Facilitator to Run Your Retreat?

ForumSherpa has a team of professional, experienced facilitators who have been certified in our methodology and programs. For a powerful, transformational retreat experience, trust the experts at ForumSherpa!

Facilitator bios and testimonials are online. To find a facilitator and/or check availability, visit **www.forumsherpa.com/meet-the-team**.

Interested in Our Retreat Programs?

Select a retreat program from ForumSherpa's extensive library of curriculum and exercises. All of our programs have been developed through years of study and analysis by experienced Forum experts. The exercises will provoke new thought perspectives and push you outside your comfort zone to places that affect real change. Most programs require preparatory work and/or assessments in advance of the retreat. All programs offer take-away value beyond the retreat itself, ensuring a high ROI for the Forum and its members. Visit **www.forumsherpa.com/retreats** for more information.

First Forum Retreat	Forums embarking on their first retreat will appreciate the structured, developmental aspects of the First Forum Retreat. This program positions a new Forum(less than two years old) for a high-value Forum experience. Member objectives are identified and aligned, and the Forum learns a common language for continued growth and development. Avoid common pitfalls that many Forums experience during their first year of existence and kick-start your Forum in the right direction!
Forum 2.0®	Forum 2.0® is the next stage of a high-value Forum experience, ideal for mature, healthy Forums. Learn a suite of new tools, processes and value boosters from around the globe, presented in a highly interactive format. It's powerful, high-energy, fun and informative. Three levels of content are introduced over a three-year period, one level per year, as the Forum advances from "Base Camp" to the "Summit". Many of the tools and processes can be applied to your corporate management team too!
Business Deep Dive	The Business Deep Dive retreat enables each member to explore their business at a deeper level and get input from the Forum on how to achieve company goals. The pre-work exercises set the stage for an intense discussion about each business, including "cloaking" by the Forum. During the retreat, members set goals and KPIs, and identify a structure for reporting and supporting each other toward success. Discussions include a tactical look at the EOS®/Traction model.
Goalkeepers™	The Goalkeepers™ Retreat is a unique opportunity to look at where you are today, decide where you want to be tomorrow, and create a road map to get there successfully! Using a proven combination of exercises, tools and techniques, participants find the clarity and commitment they need to achieve their dreams. Join the growing number of business owners, executives and success-driven individuals who have experienced this powerful program with breakthrough results!
Leadership Development	The Leadership Development Retreat provides a study of several leadership styles, traits and characteristics. The Forum engages in a series of assessments, exercises and discussions to explore the application of leadership in business. By the end of the retreat, each person has set specific goals for leadership development and created an action plan for successful execution.
Forum Health	The Forum Health Retreat is a revitalizing opportunity for your Forum to review the basics, raise meeting value and work on issues and relationships within the Forum. The retreat begins with a comprehensive Forum Health Survey that measures 87 data points of Forum Health. The retreat agenda, pre-work and on-site exercises are customized and based on the results of the survey.
Life Balance & Legacy	In today's busy, connected world, finding a balance between work, family, community and self can be daunting. Explore how balanced your life is thru a series of thought-provoking exercises, discussions and introspection. Assess your healthful habits and contemplate what you want your legacy to be. Then, embark on a journey of identifying your ideal balance, your future legacy and a plan to achieve them.

www.ingramcontent.com/pod-product-compliance
Lightning Source LLC
Chambersburg PA
CBHW080246030426
42334CB00023BA/2717